A/77/17

General Assembly
Official Records
Seventy-seventh Session
Supplement No. 17

Report of the United Nations Commission on International Trade Law

Fifty-fifth session (27 June–15 July 2022)

United Nations • New York, 2022

Note

Symbols of United Nations documents are composed of letters combined with figures. Mention of such a symbol indicates a reference to a United Nations document.

Print ISNB: 978-92-1-003418-0
e ISBN: 978-92-1-107037-8

[3 August 2022]

Contents

I. Introduction

1. The present report of the United Nations Commission on International Trade Law (UNCITRAL) covers the fifty-fifth session of the Commission, held in New York from 27 June to 15 July 2022.

2. Pursuant to General Assembly resolution 2205 (XXI) of 17 December 1966, this report is submitted to the General Assembly and is also submitted for comments to the United Nations Conference on Trade and Development (UNCTAD).

II. Organization of the session

A. Opening of the session

3. The fifty-fifth session of the Commission was opened by the Under-Secretary-General for Legal Affairs and Legal Counsel of the United Nations, Miguel de Serpa Soares, on 27 June 2022.

B. Membership and attendance

4. The General Assembly, in its resolution 2205 (XXI), established the Commission with a membership of 29 States, elected by the General Assembly. By its resolution 3108 (XXVIII) of 12 December 1973, the General Assembly increased the membership of the Commission from 29 to 36 States. By its resolution 57/20 of 19 November 2002, the General Assembly further increased the membership of the Commission from 36 States to 60 States. By its resolution 76/109 of 9 December 2021, the General Assembly increased again the membership of the Commission from 60 to 70 States. Five additional members were to be elected during the seventy-sixth session of the General Assembly, with the remaining five additional members to be elected during the seventy-ninth session of the General Assembly.

5. The current members of the Commission are the following States, whose term of office expires on the last day prior to the beginning of the annual session of the Commission in the year indicated:[1] Afghanistan (2028), Algeria (2025), Argentina (2028), Armenia (2028), Australia (2028), Austria (2028), Belarus (2028), Belgium (2025), Brazil (2028), Bulgaria (2028), Cameroon (2025), Canada (2025), Chile (2028), China (2025), Colombia (2028), Côte d'Ivoire (2025), Croatia (2025), Czechia (2028), Democratic Republic of the Congo (2028), Dominican Republic (2025), Ecuador (2025), Finland (2025), France (2025), Germany (2025), Ghana (2025), Greece (2028), Honduras (2025), Hungary (2025), India (2028), Indonesia (2025), Iran (Islamic Republic of) (2028), Iraq (2028), Israel (2028), Italy (2028), Japan (2025), Kenya (2028), Kuwait (2028), Malawi (2028), Malaysia (2025), Mali (2025), Mauritius (2028), Mexico (2025), Morocco (2028), Nigeria (2028), Panama (2028), Peru (2025), Poland (2028), Republic of Korea (2025), Russian Federation (2025), Saudi Arabia (2028), Singapore (2025), Somalia (2028), South Africa (2025), Spain (2028), Switzerland (2025), Thailand (2028), Türkiye (2028), Turkmenistan (2028), Uganda (2028), Ukraine (2025), United Kingdom of Great Britain and Northern Ireland (2025), United States of America (2028), Venezuela (Bolivarian Republic of) (2028), Viet Nam (2025) and Zimbabwe (2025).

[1] Pursuant to General Assembly resolution 2205 (XXI), the members of the Commission are elected for a term of six years. Of the current membership, 30 were elected by the Assembly on 17 December 2018, at its seventy-third session, 34 were elected by the Assembly on 15 March 2022, at its seventy-sixth session, and one was elected by the Assembly on 29 June 2022, at its seventy-sixth session. By its resolution 31/99, the Assembly altered the dates of commencement and termination of membership by deciding that members would take office at the beginning of the first day of the regular annual session of the Commission immediately following their election and that their terms of office would expire on the last day prior to the opening of the seventh regular annual session following their election.

6. With the exception of Afghanistan, Bulgaria, Colombia, Kenya, Mali, Mauritius and Somalia, all the States members of the Commission were represented at the session.

7. The session was attended by observers from the following States: Bahrain, Burkina Faso, Chad, El Salvador, Equatorial Guinea, Madagascar, Mongolia, Nepal, Niger, Philippines, Qatar, Slovakia, Slovenia, Sweden and Tunisia.

8. The session was also attended by observers from the Holy See and the European Union.

9. The session was also attended by observers from the following international organizations:

(a) United Nations system: International Maritime Organization (IMO), World Bank Group and World Maritime University;

(b) Intergovernmental organizations: Commonwealth of Independent States, Cooperation Council for the Arab States of the Gulf, European Bank for Reconstruction and Development, Hague Conference on Private International Law (HCCH), International Institute for the Unification of Private Law (UNIDROIT), Interparliamentary Assembly of Member Nations of the Commonwealth of Independent States, and Organization of American States (OAS);

(c) Invited non-governmental organizations: All India Bar Association, Beijing Arbitration Commission/Beijing International Arbitration Center, Cairo Regional Centre for International Commercial Arbitration (CRCICA), Center for International Investment and Commercial Arbitration, China Council for the Promotion of International Trade, China International Economic and Trade Arbitration Commission, Comité Français de l'Arbitrage, Comité Maritime International, Construction Industry Arbitration Council, Council of the Notariats of the European Union, European Law Institute, Factors Chain International, Georgian International Arbitration Centre, Groupe de réflexion sur l'insolvabilité et sa prévention, Hong Kong Mediation Centre, Inter-American Bar Association, Inter-American Commercial Arbitration Commission, International and Comparative Law Research Center, International Association of Young Lawyers, International Bar Association, International Chamber of Commerce (ICC), International Chamber of Shipping, International Commercial Arbitration Court at the Chamber of Commerce and Industry of Ukraine, International Dispute Resolution Institute, International Federation of Freight Forwarders Associations, International Insolvency Institute, International Institute for Sustainable Development, International Swaps and Derivatives Association, International Union of Notaries, International Women's Insolvency and Restructuring Confederation, Latin American Group of Lawyers for International Trade Law, Law Association for Asia and the Pacific, Madrid Court of Arbitration, Miami International Arbitration Society, Moot Alumni Association, National Competitiveness Center, New York City Bar Association, New York International Arbitration Center, Nigerian Institute of Chartered Arbitrators, PRIME Finance Foundation, Regional Centre for International Commercial Arbitration, Russian Arbitration Centre at the Russian Institute of Modern Arbitration and Stockholm Chamber of Commerce.

10. The Commission welcomed the participation of international non-governmental organizations with expertise in the major items on the agenda. Their participation was crucial for the quality of texts formulated by the Commission, and the Commission requested the Secretariat to continue to invite such organizations to its sessions.

C. Election of officers

11. The Commission elected the following officers:

Chair:	Ivan Šimonović (Croatia)
Vice-Chairs:	Beate Czerwenka (Germany) Eva Isabelle Eliette Niamke (Côte d'Ivoire) Suphanvasa Chotikajan Tang (Thailand)
Rapporteur:	Felipe Augusto Ramos (Brazil)

D. Agenda

12. The agenda of the fifty-fifth session of the Commission, as contained in the provisional agenda and annotations thereto (A/CN.9/1083), was adopted by the Commission at its 1157th meeting, on 27 June.

E. Establishment of the Committee of the Whole

13. The Commission established a Committee of the Whole and referred to it for consideration of agenda item 6 (on consideration of a draft model law on the use and cross-border recognition of identity management and trust services). The Commission elected Giusella Finocchiaro (Italy) to chair the Committee of the Whole. The Committee of the Whole met on 5 and 6 July 2022 and held four meetings. At its 1170th meeting, on 7 July 2022, the Commission considered and adopted the report of the Committee of the Whole and agreed to include it in the present report. (The report of the Committee of the Whole is reproduced in paragraphs 112–148 of the present report.)

F. Adoption of the report

14. The Commission adopted the present report by consensus at its 1176th and 1177th meetings, on 14 July 2022.

III. Summary of the work of the Commission at its fifty-fifth session

15. With respect to agenda item 4 (on consideration of a draft convention on the international effects of judicial sales of ships), the Commission finalized and approved the text of the draft convention, which is reproduced in annex I to the present report.

16. With respect to agenda item 5 (on consideration of draft recommendations to assist mediation centres under the UNCITRAL Mediation Rules), the Commission finalized and adopted the recommendations, which are reproduced in annex III to the present report.

17. With respect to agenda item 6 (on consideration of a draft model law on the use and cross-border recognition of identity management and trust services), the Commission finalized and adopted the Model Law, which is reproduced in annex II to the present report, and approved in principle the explanatory note thereto.

18. With respect to agenda item 7 (Progress report of working groups), the Commission took note of the progress reports of Working Group I (Micro-, Small and Medium-sized Enterprises (MSMEs)), Working Group II (Dispute Settlement), Working Group III (Investor-State Dispute Settlement Reform), Working Group IV (Electronic Commerce) and Working Group V (Insolvency Law). The Commission expressed its satisfaction with the progress made by those working groups. The work of Working Group VI (Judicial Sale of Ships) was considered under agenda item 4.

19. With respect to agenda item 8 (Coordination and cooperation), the Commission took note of the notes by the Secretariat on coordination activities and on international governmental and non-governmental organizations invited to sessions of UNCITRAL and its working groups, as well as the reports by HCCH, UNIDROIT and OAS.

20. With respect to agenda item 9 ("Endorsement of texts of other organizations: ICC's International Standard Demand Guarantee Practice for URDG 758 (ISDGP)"), the Commission endorsed the International Standard Demand Guarantee Practice for URDG 758 for worldwide use, in conjunction with URDG 758, as appropriate.

21. With respect to agenda item 10 (Secretariat reports on non-legislative activities), the Commission took note of the notes by the Secretariat concerning non-legislative activities. The Commission expressed its gratitude to States and organizations that had contributed to the UNCITRAL trust funds since the Commission's fifty-fourth session, and called upon all States, international organizations and other interested entities to consider or to continue making contributions to those trust funds. The Commission welcomed the report on the transparency repository and expressed its support for continued operation of the repository as a key mechanism for promoting transparency in investor-State arbitration. The Commission also recalled the importance of ensuring a uniform interpretation and application of its texts and reiterated its call for contributions from all legal traditions to its uniform interpretation tools. All States that enacted UNCITRAL texts were invited to nominate national correspondents for reporting relevant case law to the UNCITRAL secretariat. The Commission noted with interest the progress towards a rejuvenation of the Case Law on UNCITRAL Texts (CLOUT) system, and its focus on building a more active and productive network of CLOUT contributors and covering an expanded range of UNCITRAL texts. The Commission also noted with interest the further expansion of engagement with academic partners, geared towards young researchers and practitioners in international trade law, including the UNCITRAL Asia-Pacific Days, the UNCITRAL Latin American and Caribbean Days and the UNCITRAL Days in Africa, and noted that reports on the 2021 editions of the UNCITRAL Days were available on its website. The Commission commended the secretariat for having organized a panel discussion on technical assistance activities in the field of insolvency law.

22. With respect to agenda item 11 (Work programme of the Commission), the Commission:

(a) Confirmed the programme of current legislative activities carried out by its Working Groups I, III and V;

(b) Requested the secretariat to continue to implement the stocktaking project on dispute resolution in the digital economy, and to continue to take part in the Inclusive Global Legal Innovation Platform on Online Dispute Resolution;

(c) Entrusted Working Group II with considering the topics of technology-related dispute resolution and adjudication jointly and to develop a guidance text on early dismissal and preliminary determination, with a view to presenting it to the Commission for its consideration at its fifty-sixth session, in 2023;

(d) Agreed that Working Group IV should, as regards automated contracting:

(i) As a first stage, compile provisions of UNCITRAL texts that apply to automated contracting, and revise those provisions, as appropriate; and

(ii) As a second stage, identify and develop possible new provisions;

(e) Agreed that, as regards data provision contracts, Working Group IV should proceed on the basis of the preparatory work presented to the Commission;

(f) Requested the secretariat to prepare a guidance document on legal issues relating to the use of distributed ledger systems in trade, within existing resources, and in cooperation with other concerned organizations, as appropriate;

(g) Authorized the secretariat to publish the content of the revised taxonomy in the six official languages of the United Nations;

(h) Agreed that Working Group VI should take up work towards the development of a new instrument on negotiable multimodal transport documents;

(i) Requested the secretariat to continue exploratory work of legal issues related to the impact of the coronavirus disease (COVID-19) on international trade law;

(j) Requested the secretariat to consult with interested States with a view to developing a more detailed proposal on the topic of climate change mitigation, adaptation and resilience, for consideration by the Commission at its next session in 2023, and to organize a colloquium or an expert group meeting to be held at that same session;

(k) Noted that the Working Group on a Model Law on Warehouse Receipts, convened by UNIDROIT in consultation with the UNCITRAL secretariat, might need more than two sessions before it could submit a preliminary draft for consideration by the Governing Council of UNIDROIT, possibly in 2023, and subsequent transmittal to the first available UNCITRAL working group.

23. With respect to agenda item 12 (Date and place of future meetings), the Commission approved the holding of its fifty-sixth session in Vienna, from 3 to 21 July 2023, and the schedule for working group sessions to be held in the second half of 2022 and first half of 2023.

IV. Finalization and approval of the draft convention on the international effects of judicial sales of ships

A. Introduction

24. The Commission recalled the decision made at its fifty-first session (New York, 25 June–13 July 2018), to assign the topic of the judicial sale of ships to Working Group VI,[2] which commenced its deliberations on the topic at its thirty-fifth session (New York, 13–17 May 2019). At its fifty-second session (Vienna, 8–19 July 2019),[3] the Commission expressed its satisfaction with the progress that had been made by the Working Group at its thirty-fifth session. At its resumed fifty-third session, (Vienna (online), 14–18 September 2020), the Commission considered the work of the Working Group at its thirty-sixth session and confirmed that the Working Group should continue its work to prepare an international instrument on the topic.[4] At the fifty-fourth session of the Commission (Vienna, 28 June–16 July 2021), satisfaction was expressed with the progress made by the Working Group at its thirty-seventh and thirty-eighth sessions.[5]

25. At the present session, the Commission had before it the reports of Working Group VI on the work of its thirty-ninth session (Vienna, 18–22 October 2021) (A/CN.9/1089) and its fortieth session (New York, 7–11 February 2022) (A/CN.9/1095). It also had before it the text of the draft convention on the international effects of judicial sales of ships (A/CN.9/1108, annex) and a compilation of comments submitted by States and relevant international organizations on the draft convention (A/CN.9/1109, A/CN.9/1109/Add.1, A/CN.9/1109/Add.2 and A/CN.9/1109/Add.3).

26. The Commission heard that the secretariat had prepared a draft explanatory note on the draft convention (A/CN.9/1110, A/CN.9/1110/Add.1 and A/CN.9/1110/Add.2), which was before the Commission for its information. It was emphasized that, in accordance with UNCITRAL practice, the Commission would not be called upon to approve the explanatory note. The explanatory note was a secretariat document that would be updated to reflect the deliberations of the Commission and text of the draft convention as approved.

[2] *Official Records of the General Assembly, Seventy-third session, Supplement No. 17* (A/73/17), para. 252.

[3] Ibid., *Seventy-fourth session, Supplement No. 17* (A/74/17), para. 189.

[4] Ibid., *Seventy-fifth session, Supplement No. 17* (A/75/17), part two, paras. 47 and 51 (f).

[5] Ibid., *Seventy-sixth session, Supplement No. 17* (A/76/17), para. 211.

B. Consideration of the draft convention

27. The Commission agreed to proceed with an article-by-article read-through of the draft convention, starting with article 1.

Article 1

28. The Commission heard a proposal to amend article 1 by inserting the word "international" before "effects". It was acknowledged that the amendment aligned article 1 with the title of the draft convention and better reflected its focus. It was explained that the amendment did not mean that the provisions of the convention could not apply in domestic cases; for instance, it did not mean that, for a judicial sale of a ship that was registered in the State of judicial sale, no certificate of judicial sale would be issued under article 5, that no action was required to be taken by the registrar under article 7 or that the prohibition on arrest under article 8 did not apply. On that understanding, which would be clarified in the explanatory note, the Commission approved article 1 with that amendment.

29. The Commission did not take up a proposal to incorporate article 1 into article 3, noting that the interaction between article 1 and article 3 had been considered at length by the Working Group.

Article 2

30. The Commission heard several proposals to amend the definition of "judicial sale" in article 2, subparagraph (a). The Commission did not agree to insert the words "conducted in accordance with the law of the State of judicial sale" at the end of the chapeau of article 2, subparagraph (a), confirming the decision of the Working Group to avoid dealing with substantive issues in the definitions. A proposal to refer not only to sale by public auction but also to sale by public tender was also not taken up. While it was noted that an auction was different to a tender process, and that the convention applied to both means of sale, it was felt that it was sufficient for the explanatory note to state that the reference in article 2, subparagraph (a) (i), to a sale by "public auction" included a sale by public tender. The Commission did not take up a proposal to amend the definition of "judicial sale" to incorporate a requirement that the judicial sale result from a claim asserted against the ship (and not against the shipowner in personam).

31. In response to a query as to the exact meaning of the term, the Commission noted that "private treaty sales" ordinarily resulted from arrangements normally between the mortgagee and the prospective purchaser that were approved by the court of judicial sale, and that the name and procedure for such sales differed among the States whose law accommodated them.

32. The Commission heard a proposal to include a new definition of "completion of judicial sale" to clarify that it meant that the sale "is not subject to a review in the State of judicial sale and that, according to the law of that State, the time limit for seeking ordinary review has expired". While some support was expressed for the proposal, several concerns were raised. First, it was recalled that the Working Group had considered the issue at length and had concluded that the convention should not define the term in deference to the law of the State of judicial sale. Second, it was noted that the proposal was not about finding a harmonized understanding of when a judicial sale was "completed", but rather about helping to determine when the certificate of judicial sale would be issued in the State of judicial sale. It was further observed that the wording of the proposal was drawn from article 4, paragraph 4, of the Convention on the Recognition and Enforcement of Foreign Judgments in Civil or Commercial Matters (2019), where it was used to determine when a foreign judgment was amenable to recognition and enforcement. It was noted that the review of a judicial sale was substantively different to the review of a judgment, particularly insofar as it concerned a measure to enforce a judgment, and that there was likely greater disparity between the kinds of recourse available to challenge a judicial sale, many of which might have long limitation periods.

33. The Commission approved article 2 without amendment.

Article 3

34. The Commission agreed to amend article 3, paragraph 1, by formulating subparagraphs (a) and (b) in the present tense. Accordingly, it agreed to replace the words "was" with "is". It also agreed to refer to the time of "that" sale.

35. The Commission heard a proposal to insert the words "as determined by the law of the State of judicial sale" at the end of article 3, paragraph 1 (b). It was explained that the proposal was designed to find a more appropriate place for the existing requirement in article 4, paragraph 1, for the time of judicial sale to be determined in accordance with the law of the State of judicial sale. However, it was observed that the proposed words might give rise to ambiguity insofar as it was not clear whether it was the physical location of the ship or the time of judicial sale that would be determined by the law of the State of judicial sale or whether the ship would need to be physically located in the State of judicial sale at the time of the judicial sale and not only at an earlier stage (e.g. at the time of arrest). The Commission did not take up the proposal.

36. The Commission approved article 3 with the amendments outlined above (para. 34).

Article 4 and annex I

37. The Commission approved article 4, paragraph 1, without amendment.

38. The Commission did not take up a proposal to include a requirement for the notice of judicial sale to be given "in due time". It also heard that requiring the notice to be given prior to the judicial sale could be problematic if the judicial sale were understood to be a process that commenced at the beginning of the procedure, before the time at which notices were ordinarily given. The Commission did not take up a proposal to amend article 4, paragraph 2, to refer instead to giving notice prior to the public auction or conclusion of the private treaty and instead approved article 4, paragraph 2, without amendment.

39. The Commission did not take up a drafting suggestion to recast paragraphs 3 to 7 of article 4 as subparagraphs of article 4, paragraph 3, so as to reinforce that those provisions did not serve as stand-alone obligations but rather as conditions for the issuance of the certificate of judicial sale under article 5.

40. The Commission agreed to amend article 4, paragraph 3, to refer to the "registry" on the basis that the registry is the entity that is capable of receiving notice. The Commission approved article 4, paragraph 3, with that amendment. It confirmed that article 4, paragraph 3 (d), as well as article 5, paragraph 2 (h), and item 5 of the model certificate of judicial sale contained in annex II to the draft convention, should refer to "owner" in the singular, on the basis that: (a) according to United Nations drafting style, the singular included the plural; and (b) the definition of "owner" made it clear that more than one person may be the owner of a ship. The Commission did not take up a proposal to include a requirement to notify the embassy or consulate of the State of registration. It was stressed that article 4 imposed minimum requirements and did not prevent the law of the State of judicial sale from specifying other persons to be notified.

41. For consistency, the Commission agreed to amend article 4, paragraph 4, to delete the words "to this Convention" and approved the paragraph as amended. The Commission approved article 4, paragraph 5, without amendment.

42. The Commission engaged in a detailed discussion about the language requirement in article 4, paragraph 6. It was recalled that the provision originated in a proposal to apply a language requirement to the notice of judicial sale whenever given, but that the subsequent revision of the text to specify the target language as one of the working languages of the repository had shifted focus to applying the language requirement only when the notice was given to the repository. There was broad support for the view that, if the intention was to apply the language requirement only when the notice was given

to the repository, the words "for the purpose of communicating the notice to the repository" should be inserted to article 4, paragraph 6. The Commission agreed that the language requirement should be so applied and accordingly agreed to insert the proposed words. The Commission approved article 4, paragraph 6, as amended. It also agreed that the explanatory note should be revised to encourage the person giving notice, as a matter of good practice, to consider translating the minimum information for the purpose of giving the notice under article 4, paragraph 3, particularly given that that information would eventually need to be translated for the purposes of transmitting the notice to the repository.

43. The Commission heard a proposal to delete the word "exclusively" in article 4, paragraph 7, out of concern that the provision would otherwise limit the sources of information that the person giving notice could use. There was broad agreement that that was not the intention of the provision. As an alternative, it was suggested to replace the words "reliance may exclusively be placed on" with words such as "it is sufficient to place reliance on". The Commission agreed to the alternative formulation "it is sufficient to rely on" and approved article 4, paragraph 7, without further amendment.

44. The Commission did not take up a proposal to require confirmation of receipt by the person being notified.

45. The Commission agreed to amend annex I to the draft convention to clarify that all references to a "sale" were to the "judicial sale" and approved annex I without further amendment. The Commission did not take up a proposal to insert a requirement for a follow-up notice to be given if, at the time that the original notice is given, only the anticipated date, time or place of public auction is known. It also did not take up a proposal to revise annex I to accommodate sales by public tender, for the reasons given above (para. 30) or to supplement item 12 to provide more explicit information about challenging the judicial sale (including information on the court competent under article 9), a matter on which the Working Group had previously deliberated.

Article 5 and annex II

46. The Commission agreed to amend article 5, paragraph 1, to refer to the "other" public authority. It did not take up a suggestion to address situations in which two certificates of judicial sale were circulating for the same ship. It agreed to amend article 5, paragraph 2 (b), to refer to "a statement that the judicial sale has conferred clean title to the ship on the purchaser" and to amend subparagraph (b) of the model certificate of judicial sale contained in annex II to align it with article 5, paragraph 2 (b).

47. The Commission engaged in a detailed discussion as to whether article 5, paragraph 2 (e), should refer to the court or other public authority "ordering, approving or confirming" the judicial sale rather than the court "conducting" the sale. It was recalled that annex I and annex II were relevant at different times and that, while it might be relevant to distinguish between the court or other authority "ordering, approving or confirming" the judicial sale at the time at which notice is given, it was not necessary to do so at the time that the certificate of judicial sale is issued, which only occurred upon completion of the judicial sale. At the same time, it was also observed that the authority conducting the judicial sale might be different to the authority ordering, approving or confirming the sale. After discussion, the Commission agreed to keep the reference to "conducted" in article 5, paragraph 2 (e), and to amend item 3.1 of the model certificate of judicial sale contained in annex II to align it with article 5, paragraph 2 (e). The Commission also agreed to replace the words "ordered, approved or confirmed" with "conducted" in article 5, paragraph 1.

48. A query was raised about the meaning of article 5, paragraph 2 (k). It was explained that "other confirmation of authenticity of the certificate" included a seal but could also cover the means used to issue electronic certificates.

49. The Commission accepted a proposal to amend article 5, paragraph 4, to insert the words "and any translation thereof" after the words "judicial sale".

50. Recalling its deliberations on the word "owner" (see para. 40 above), the Commission approved article 5 and annex II without further amendment.

Article 6

51. The Commission approved article 6 without amendment.

Article 7

52. Recalling its earlier deliberations on article 4, paragraph 3 (see para. 40 above), the Commission agreed to refer to "registry" rather than "registrar" throughout the convention, but to retain references to the "register" as the record maintained by the registry.

53. The Commission considered a proposal to amend the chapeau of article 7, paragraph 1, with respect to requests by subsequent purchasers by (a) deleting the words "or subsequent purchaser" and (b) inserting, after "article 5", the words "or at the request of the subsequent purchaser and upon production of the certificate and further documentation on the transfer of ownership from the purchaser to the subsequent purchaser". There was general agreement that a subsequent purchaser should be required to demonstrate its entitlement to request any particular action by the registry and, for that purpose, also be required to submit such additional documents or evidence as the registry may require under its regulations and procedures. However, several concerns were expressed about the proposal. First, it was stated that the requirement was already covered by the allowance for the registry (or other competent authority) to take action "in accordance with its regulations and procedures". Second, it was stated that, for those jurisdictions in which a transfer of ownership occurred upon registration of the new owner, it made no sense to require production of documentation on the transfer of ownership. It was added that, in any case, such a requirement would be problematic, as the draft convention did not address ownership.

54. The Commission agreed that it was preferable to address the issue in the explanatory note and invited the secretariat to revise the draft explanatory note to acknowledge that the regulations and procedures of the registry extended to the manner in which an applicant established that it had purchased the ship from the purchaser, and thus qualified as a "subsequent purchaser".

55. The Commission agreed to amend article 7, paragraph 1 (a), by inserting the words "from the register" after "delete". It also agreed to delete the word "or" at the end of article 7, paragraph 1 (c), as the non-cumulative nature of the actions to be taken by the registry was already established by the words "as the case may be" in the chapeau of article 7, paragraph 1, and the requirement for the registry to act "at the request of the purchaser or subsequent purchaser".

56. The Commission approved article 7, paragraph 1, without any further amendment.

57. The Commission approved article 7, paragraphs 2 and 3. It was proposed to delete article 7, paragraph 4, on the basis that the registry could readily make its own copy of the certificate of judicial sale for its records. The Commission decided to retain the provision and approved article 7, paragraph 4, without amendment.

58. The Commission agreed to amend article 7, paragraph 5, by inserting the words "of the" before "other competent authority" to clarify that the provision was concerned only with the determination by a court, and then only with the court in the State in which the action under article 7, paragraphs 1 or 2, was taken (i.e. action by the registry or other competent authority). The Commission approved article 7, paragraph 5, with that amendment.

Article 8

59. The Commission agreed to amend article 8, paragraphs 1 and 2, by replacing "an earlier judicial sale" with "a judicial sale" and approved those paragraphs with those

amendments. The Commission approved article 8, paragraphs 3 and 4, without amendment.

Article 9

60. The Commission heard that the Working Group had previously considered, but not taken up, a proposal to amend article 9 to require the State of judicial sale to provide for adequate remedies to challenge a judicial sale. The importance of such a provision as a means to safeguard the legitimate interests of creditors by affording them the opportunity to assert their rights was stressed. It was conceded that the provision should be separated from article 9 so that the latter would deal solely with jurisdiction.

61. In response, it was pointed out that the notion of "adequacy" was vague and that the provision went against the objective of the convention to leave matters of procedure related to judicial sales to domestic law. Moreover, it raised questions about the consequences of breach. Specifically, a concern was raised that the provision could support the argument that the adequacy of remedies in the State of judicial sale was a matter of public policy in any State asked to give effect to a foreign sale, which in turn could lead to foreign courts seized under article 10 scrutinizing foreign judicial acts and ultimately standing in judgment of the courts of the State of judicial sale. In that regard, it was suggested that the provision might be more problematic than an alternative proposal put to the Commission to amend article 10 so as to state that public policy included circumstances in which "the specific proceedings leading to the issuance of the certificate were incompatible with fundamental principles of procedural fairness" of the State addressed.

62. As a compromise, the Commission heard a proposal to amend article 4, paragraph 1, to refer to procedures for challenging the judicial sale. Broad support was expressed for the proposal, and the Commission agreed to recast article 4, paragraph 1, as follows:

> "The judicial sale shall be conducted in accordance with the law of the State of judicial sale, which shall also provide procedures for challenging the judicial sale prior to its completion and determine the time of the sale for the purposes of this Convention."

63. It was understood that the provision did not require a State party to introduce or devise new legislation providing specific procedures for challenging a judicial sale, and that it would be sufficient for the State to point to procedures under existing law, whether provided for in legislation, rules of civil procedure, or case law, and whether or not specific to judicial sales. The secretariat was invited to revise the draft explanatory note to explicitly state that understanding and to indicate that the requirements of article 4, paragraph 1, would be met whenever a State seeking to become party to the Convention satisfied itself that adequate procedures were in place consistent with its constitutional framework. It was added that most States would ordinarily have procedures in place for challenging a judicial sale.

64. Returning to article 9, the Commission agreed to delete the comma before "for which a certificate has been issued in accordance with article 5, paragraph 1" as those words qualified the decisions that were to be transmitted to the repository. The Commission approved article 9 with that amendment.

Article 10

65. A proposal to delete the word "manifestly" in article 10 was not taken up, and the Commission noted that the issue had been considered at length by the Working Group.

Article 11

66. The Commission agreed to amend article 11, paragraph 3, to specify that it applies only prior to the entry into force of the Convention for the State concerned. The Commission approved article 11 with that amendment, for which the secretariat was invited to prepare a concrete drafting proposal.

Article 12

67. The Commission approved article 12, paragraph 1, without amendment. It was explained that one consequence of article 12, paragraph 1, was that the authorities of States parties could correspond directly without needing to resort to diplomatic channels.

68. The Commission agreed to amend article 12, paragraph 2, and other provisions of the convention by replacing "international convention, treaty or agreement" with "international agreement". It also agreed to replace "affects" with "shall affect the application of" in order to maintain consistency with the formulation used in article 13, paragraph 1. The Commission approved article 12 with those amendments to paragraph 2.

Article 13

69. The Commission accepted a proposal to use lower case when referring to another convention other than by its full title. The Commission approved article 13, paragraph 1, without further amendment. The Commission did not take up a proposal to delete article 13, paragraph 2, and approved it without further amendment. The secretariat was invited to revise the explanatory note to state that a State party may need to amend its laws to divert the notice of judicial sale from the channels of transmission provided under the Convention on the Service Abroad of Judicial and Extrajudicial Documents in Civil or Commercial Matters (1965).

Article 14

70. The Commission agreed to amend article 14 by replacing the words "preclude any basis for giving effect in one State" with the words "preclude a State Party from giving effect". It was observed that the amendment did not change the substance of the provision. Recalling its deliberations on using the words "international agreement" (see para. 68 above), the Commission approved article 14 with those amendments.

Article 15

71. The Commission approved article 15 without amendment.

Article 16

72. The Commission approved article 16 without amendment.

Article 17

73. The Commission heard an offer from the Government of China to organize a ceremony for the signing of the convention in Beijing, once adopted, and a proposal to refer to the convention as the "Beijing Convention" in an abbreviated form. The Commission was informed that the Government of China was prepared to assume the additional costs that might be incurred by the convening of a signing ceremony outside the premises of the United Nations so that the organization of the signing ceremony would not require additional resources under the United Nations budget.

74. The Commission expressed its gratitude for the offer of the Government of China to host a signing ceremony and there was wide support for recommending that the General Assembly accept that offer and that the convention be known as the "Beijing Convention on the Judicial Sale of Ships". Concerns were expressed about the possible impact of the COVID-19 pandemic, as well as the measures that the host country might take to combat it, on the organization and timing of the signing ceremony, in particular on the ability of foreign representatives to travel to Beijing without being subject to quarantine. It was noted that a fallback option would be to have the convention open for signature at United Nations Headquarters only. In response, it was observed that the Government of China monitored closely the evolution of the pandemic and adjusted its strategies accordingly. It was noted that, in any event, several months would be needed after the adoption of the convention by the General Assembly, to allow for appropriate arrangements to be made as between the depositary and the host Government to address

concerns about the impact of the pandemic on the signing ceremony. It was noted that it was not necessary for the Commission to have agreed on a date for the signing ceremony prior to transmitting the draft convention to the General Assembly.

75. The Commission agreed to amend article 17, paragraph 1, by inserting the word "Beijing" within the first set of square brackets and to leave the second set of square brackets blank. The Commission approved article 17, paragraph 1, with that amendment, as well as the remainder of article 17.

Article 18

76. The Commission agreed to amend the final sentence of article 18, paragraph 1, by correcting the cross references to the articles of the convention on entry into force and amendment, respectively, and by inserting at the end of the sentence the words "in addition to the instruments deposited by its member States".

77. The Commission approved article 18, paragraph 2, subject to consequential amendments resulting from the insertion of the common clause on declarations (see the section on art. 21 below). The Commission approved article 18, paragraph 3, without amendment.

78. The Commission approved the insertion of the following "disconnection clause" as a new paragraph 4:

> "This Convention shall not affect the application of the rules of a regional economic integration organization, whether adopted before or after this Convention:
>
> (a) In relation to the transmission of a notice of judicial sale between member States of such an organization; or
>
> (b) In relation to the jurisdictional rules applicable between member States of such an organization."

Article 19

79. The Commission approved article 19, paragraph 1, subject to consequential amendments resulting from the insertion of the common clause on declarations (see the section on art. 21 below). The Commission also agreed to delete article 19, paragraph 2, on the basis that amendments to declarations were addressed in that clause. The Commission approved the remainder of article 19 without amendment.

Article 20

80. The Commission heard that article 20 was a new provision that had been drafted by the secretariat in response to a request by the Working Group at its fortieth session (A/CN.9/1108, para. 6). It was explained that the provision, which gave States parties the option to apply the Convention Abolishing the Requirement of Legalisation for Foreign Public Documents (1961) (Apostille Convention) with respect to foreign certificates of judicial sale, represented a compromise between article 5, paragraph 4, which exempted the certificate of judicial sale from legalization or similar formality, and concerns about the willingness of registry officials in some States to take action on a foreign certificate of judicial sale without assurances of its authenticity, which in turn might limit the appeal of the convention to those States.

81. Some support was expressed for retaining the provision. It was noted that the Apostille Convention was in force in over 120 States, which meant that the formality under the Convention, that is, the addition of an apostille certificate, was widely accepted as a means to authenticate the certificate of judicial sale. Several arguments were advanced for deleting the provision. First, it was noted that the addition of an apostille did not itself authenticate the underlying document or guarantee that the underlying document was not fraudulent. Second, it was noted that the authority to which a certificate of judicial sale was provided had other means to satisfy itself as to the authenticity of the certificate, including by verifying the issuance of the certificate

in communication with the issuing authority under article 12 or by consulting the repository. Third, it was noted that the provision went against the trend in recent treaties of including the formality under the Apostille Convention within the scope of the legalization exemption. Fourth, it was noted that the provision would have the peculiar effect of subjecting States that were party to the Apostille Convention to more onerous formalities regarding legalization than States that were not party thereto, which was at odds with the very objective of the Apostille Convention to simplify those formalities. The view was also expressed that the Apostille Convention did not apply to public documents in electronic form; another view was that article 20 might undermine the acceptance of electronic certificates, as mandated by article 5, paragraph 7.

82. After discussion, the Commission agreed to delete article 20 and to renumber the remaining articles of the convention accordingly.

Article 21 (renumbered as article 20)

83. The Commission heard that article 21 was another new provision that had been drafted by the secretariat to provide a common clause dealing with how declarations under the convention were made and took effect. It was explained that the provision was based on similar clauses in other conventions prepared by the Commission.

84. The Commission agreed to retain the new provision and therefore to delete the words in square brackets in articles 18, paragraph 2, and 19, paragraph 1, which dealt with the timing and receipt of declarations. It further agreed to amend article 21, paragraphs 1 and 4, to specify the declarations to which they applied.

85. A query was raised as to whether the second sentence of article 21, paragraph 3, was needed, given that article 21, paragraph 1, provided for declarations to be made only prior to entry into force of the convention in respect of the State concerned. The Commission agreed to delete the sentence and approved the paragraph without further amendment.

86. The Commission accepted a proposal for the time periods specified in articles 21, 22, 23 and 24 to be measured in days rather than months, for added certainty, and therefore agreed to retain the corresponding option presented in square brackets in each of those articles.

87. The Commission heard a proposal to amend article 21, paragraph 4, to specify that a modification or withdrawal of a declaration notified before the entry into force of the convention for the declaring State took effect simultaneously with the entry into force of the convention for that State. It was noted that, under the treaty practice of some States, there was a possibility that the Government might wish to extend the convention to additional territorial units after depositing the instrument of ratification and initial declaration under article 19, paragraph 1, but before the convention entered into force for the State, and that a delayed entry into force for the additional territorial units could pose difficulties. Noting that the so-called "federal clause" was of particular relevance to a limited number of States, the Commission agreed to amend article 21, paragraph 4, by inserting the following sentence at the end of the paragraph:

> "If the depositary receives the notification of the modification or withdrawal before entry into force of this Convention in respect of the State concerned, the modification or withdrawal shall take effect simultaneously with the entry into force of this Convention in respect of that State."

Article 22 (renumbered as article 21)

88. The Commission agreed to retain the requirement for the deposit of three instruments of ratification, acceptance, approval or accession to bring the convention into force. It was added that a higher number was not necessary, as the convention could already start fulfilling its objective once it was in force in the State of judicial sale and in any other State expected to give effect to the judicial sale. It was therefore agreed to remove the square brackets around the word "third" in article 22, paragraph 1. The Commission approved article 22, paragraph 1, without further amendment.

89. The Commission agreed to amend the first sentence of article 22, paragraph 2, to refer to the "third" instrument of ratification, acceptance, approval or accession, and approved the provision with that amendment. Subsequently, the Commission agreed to delete the final sentence of article 22, paragraph 2, on the basis that the matter was now sufficiently addressed in article 21 as amended.

90. The Commission heard that the word "conducted" was vague and considered alternative proposals, such as to refer to when the sale was "initiated" or when the certificate of judicial sale was issued. The former proposal was considered imprecise, as it might extend back to the time of the initial arrest of the ship leading to the judicial sale. The latter proposal, in turn, was felt to be inappropriate, as it might create an obligation for States parties to give effect even to judicial sales wholly conducted prior to the entry into force of the convention, and to which the safeguards of article 4, for instance, did not apply. After discussion, the Commission agreed to focus on the specific court action triggering the judicial sale, as specified in the definition in article 2, subparagraph (a), and decided to replace "conducted" with the words "ordered or approved". The Commission approved article 22, paragraph 3, with that amendment. It was added that it was unnecessary to refer to a sale that was "confirmed", as the provision was concerned with the early stages of the judicial sale procedure and not with the final stages.

Article 23 (renumbered as article 22)

91. The Commission approved article 23, paragraphs 1, 2, 3 and 5, without amendment.

92. The Commission agreed to remove the square brackets around the word "third" and to delete the words "to the Convention" in article 23, paragraph 4. It heard a proposal to insert the word "only" after the word "binding". It was explained that the insertion was not necessary, as, in the current wording of the provision, the adopted amendment would only be binding on those States parties that had expressed consent to be bound by it. Accordingly, the Commission did not take up the proposal and approved article 23, paragraph 4, without further amendment.

Article 24 (renumbered as article 23)

93. The Commission agreed to amend the heading of article 24 to refer to "denunciation" (in the singular) and to amend the final sentence of article 24, paragraph 2, to refer to "this Convention". The Commission approved the provision with those amendments.

Preamble

94. The Commission approved the first and third paragraphs of the preamble without amendment.

95. The Commission heard several proposals to amend the second paragraph of the preamble. The first proposal was to refer to claims "against ships" or to claims "against shipowners". It was noted that judicial sales were used to enforce claims against other parties (e.g. bareboat charterers) and that it was not desirable in the preamble to limit the scope of claims. The second proposal was to refer to "claims" instead of "maritime claims". While it was acknowledged that the term "maritime claims" was widely understood and used in maritime law conventions, it was pointed out that judicial sales could be used for other claims, such as claims in insolvency. The third proposal was to refer to judicial sales not only as a means to enforce, but also as a means to "secure", a claim, as exemplified by the use of judicial sales pendente lite to maximize the proceeds available for a deteriorating asset. However, it was queried whether it was appropriate to characterize a judicial sale as "securing" a claim, which might lead to confusion with the concept of "security".

96. After discussion, the Commission agreed to refer to "claims" instead of "maritime claims" and approved the second paragraph of the preamble in the following terms:

"*Mindful* of the crucial role of shipping in international trade and transportation, of the high economic value of ships used in both seagoing and inland navigation, and of the function of judicial sales as a means to enforce claims,".

97. The Commission agreed to amend the fourth paragraph of the preamble to use terms defined in the convention, and approved the paragraph in the following terms:

"*Wishing*, for that purpose, to establish uniform rules that promote the dissemination of information on prospective judicial sales to interested parties and give international effects to judicial sales of ships sold free and clear of any mortgage or *hypothèque* and of any charge, including for ship registration purposes,".

C. Explanatory note

98. The Commission exchanged views on the content of the draft explanatory note, on the understanding that the explanatory note was a secretariat document that the Commission was not called on to approve or adopt. The Commission expressed its appreciation to the secretariat for having prepared the draft explanatory note, recalling that the secretariat would update it to reflect the deliberations during the present session and the text of the draft convention as approved. The Commission requested the secretariat to publish the revised text of the explanatory note in all official languages of the United Nations, both in electronic and printed form, and to circulate it widely, along with the text of the convention.

D. Approval of the draft convention

99. At its 1164th meeting, on 30 June 2022, the Commission adopted by consensus the following decision and recommendation to the General Assembly:

"*The United Nations Commission on International Trade Law*,

"*Recalling* its mandate under General Assembly resolution 2205 (XXI) of 17 December 1966 to further the progressive harmonization and unification of the law of international trade and in that respect to bear in mind the interests of all peoples, in particular those of developing countries, in the extensive development of international trade,

"*Mindful* of the crucial role of shipping in international trade and transportation, of the high economic value of ships used in both seagoing and inland navigation, and of the function of judicial sales as a means to enforce claims,

"*Considering* that adequate legal protection for purchasers may positively impact the price realized at judicial sales of ships, to the benefit of both shipowners and creditors, including lienholders and ship financiers,

"*Wishing*, for that purpose, to establish uniform rules that promote the dissemination of information on prospective judicial sales to interested parties and give international effects to judicial sales of ships sold free and clear of any mortgage or *hypothèque* and of any charge, including for ship registration purposes,

"*Convinced* that the adoption of a convention on the international effects of judicial sales of ships that is acceptable to States with different legal, social and economic systems would complement the existing international legal framework on shipping and navigation and contribute to the development of harmonious international economic relations,

"*Noting* that the preparation of the draft convention on the international effects of judicial sales of ships was the subject of due deliberation in the Commission and that the draft convention benefited from consultations with

Governments and interested intergovernmental and international non-governmental organizations,

"*Noting also* that the text of the draft convention was circulated for comment before the fifty-fifth session of the Commission to all Governments invited to attend the meetings of the Commission and its Working Group VI (Judicial Sale of Ships) as members and observers,

"*Having considered* the draft convention and the comments submitted by Governments and international organizations at its fifty-fifth session, in 2022,

"1. *Submits* to the General Assembly the draft convention on the international effects of judicial sales of ships, as it appears in annex I to the report of the United Nations Commission on International Trade Law on the work of its fifty-fifth session;

"2. *Recommends* that the General Assembly, taking into account the extensive consideration given to the draft convention by the Commission and its Working Group VI (Judicial Sale of Ships), consider the draft convention with a view to: (a) adopting, at its seventy-seventh session, on the basis of the draft convention approved by the Commission, the United Nations Convention on the International Effects of Judicial Sales of Ships; (b) authorizing a signing ceremony to be held as soon as practicable in 2023 in Beijing, upon which occasion the Convention would be open for signature; and (c) recommending that the Convention be known as the "Beijing Convention on the Judicial Sale of Ships";

"3. *Requests* the Secretary-General to publish the Convention, upon adoption, including electronically and in the six official languages of the United Nations, and to disseminate it broadly to Governments and other interested bodies."

V. Finalization and adoption of recommendations to assist mediation centres under the UNCITRAL Mediation Rules

A. Background

100. The Commission recalled that, at its fifty-fourth session, in 2021, it had adopted the UNCITRAL Mediation Rules[6] (the Mediation Rules) and mandated the secretariat to prepare recommendations to assist mediation institutions on how to adjust the rules for their use, which would facilitate the Mediation Rules serving as a model for institutional rules.[7]

101. The Commission was informed that, pursuant to that mandate, the secretariat, in consultation with mediation centres and experts from various parts of the world, had prepared draft recommendations to assist mediation centres and other interested bodies with regard to mediation under the UNCITRAL Mediation Rules (2021). The Commission noted that the draft recommendations followed an approach similar to the one taken in the recommendations to assist arbitral institutions and other interested bodies with regard to arbitration under the UNCITRAL Arbitration Rules (as revised in 2010), which were adopted by the Commission at its forty-fifth session, in 2012.[8]

[6] *Official Records of the General Assembly, Seventy-sixth Session, Supplement No. 17* (A/76/17), para. 101.

[7] Ibid., para. 100.

[8] Ibid., *Sixty-seventh Session, Supplement No. 17* (A/67/17), para. 64.

B. Consideration of the draft recommendations

102. The Commission considered the draft recommendations transmitted to it by the Secretariat in chapter II of document A/CN.9/1118.

103. With regard to the text in italics found in paragraph 9 of the draft recommendations, which sets out a possible amendment that mediation centres and other interested bodies might decide to introduce to article 1, paragraph 4, of the Mediation Rules, considering that requiring the consent of the mediator might be too high a threshold, it was agreed to combine the first two sentences in that text as follows: "The parties may agree in writing, in consultation with the mediator where one has been appointed, to exclude or vary any provision of the [*name of the institutional rules*] at any time." It was further suggested that the word "approach" in the last sentence should be replaced by the word "policy" to clarify that an institution should not easily decline to administer a mediation, but only when the suggested change was contrary to the policy of that institution. That suggestion did not receive support.

104. With regard to the text in italics found in paragraph 10 of the draft recommendations, which sets out a possible amendment that mediation centres and other interested bodies might decide to introduce to article 2, paragraph 2, of the Mediation Rules, a suggestion to replace the word "may" in the second sentence with the word "shall" did not receive support.

105. With regard to the text in italics found in paragraph 17 of the draft recommendations, which sets out a possible amendment that mediation centres and other interested bodies might decide to introduce to article 8, paragraph 2, of the Mediation Rules, it was agreed that the word "may" should be replaced with the word "shall" in view of the requirements of article 4 of the United Nations Convention on International Settlement Agreements Resulting from Mediation (the Singapore Convention on Mediation).[9]

106. Subject to those changes (see paras. 103 and 105 above), the Commission approved the draft recommendations.

107. It was emphasized that the recommendations to assist mediation centres and other interested bodies with regard to mediation under the UNCITRAL Mediation Rules were intended to provide guidance and were non-binding, and that the institutions would have the flexibility to further adapt the Mediation Rules. It was further highlighted that such recommendations, upon their adoption by UNCITRAL, would help to further promote mediation as a useful dispute resolution method.

C. Adoption of the recommendations to assist mediation centres and other interested bodies with regard to mediation under the UNCITRAL Mediation Rules

108. At its 1173rd meeting, on 11 July 2022, the Commission adopted by consensus the following decision:

"*The United Nations Commission on International Trade Law*,

"*Recognizing* the value of dispute settlement methods referred to by expressions such as mediation, conciliation and expressions of similar import, as a means of amicably settling disputes arising in the context of international commercial relations,

"*Noting* that such dispute settlement methods are increasingly used in international and domestic commercial practice as an alternative to litigation,

[9] General Assembly resolution 73/198, annex.

"*Considering* that the use of such dispute settlement methods results in significant benefits, such as reducing the instances where a dispute leads to the termination of a commercial relationship, facilitating the administration of international transactions by commercial parties and producing savings in the administration of justice by States,

"*Recalling* General Assembly resolutions 35/52 of 4 December 1980 and 76/107 of 9 December 2021, on the Conciliation Rules and the Mediation Rules of the United Nations Commission on International Trade Law, respectively,

"*Convinced* that recommendations to assist mediation centres and other interested bodies with regard to mediation under the UNCITRAL Mediation Rules, acceptable to mediation centres and other interested bodies in countries with different legal, social and economic systems, would complement the existing legal framework on international mediation by informing and assisting mediation centres and other interested bodies that envisage using the UNCITRAL Mediation Rules in the institutional context,

"1. *Adopts* the recommendations to assist mediation centres and other interested bodies with regard to mediation under the UNCITRAL Mediation Rules as they appear in annex III to the report of the United Nations Commission on International Trade Law on the work of its fifty-fifth session;

"2. *Invites* mediation centres and other interested bodies to consider the recommendations when adapting the UNCITRAL Mediation Rules for use in the institutional context and invites parties to make use of the UNCITRAL Mediation Rules so adapted in the settlement of disputes arising in the context of international commercial relations;

"3. *Requests* the Secretary-General to publish the recommendations, including electronically, in the six official languages of the United Nations, and to disseminate them broadly to Governments and other interested bodies."

VI. Finalization and adoption of the UNCITRAL Model Law on the Use and Cross-border Recognition of Identity Management and Trust Services

A. Background

109. It was recalled that, at its forty-ninth session, in 2016, the Commission had agreed that the topic of identity management and trust services should be retained on the agenda of Working Group IV.[10] The Working Group worked on the topic from its fifty-fifth to its sixty-third session.

110. At its sixty-second session (Vienna, 22–26 November 2021), the Working Group requested the secretariat to revise draft provisions on identity management and trust services and their explanatory note to reflect its deliberations and decisions at that session and to transmit the revised text to the Commission, in the form of a model law, for consideration at its fifty-fifth session.[11] Recalling UNCITRAL practice, the Working Group also requested the secretariat to circulate the text to all Governments and relevant international organizations for comment.[12]

111. The Commission had before it the text of the draft model law on the use and cross-border recognition of identity management and trust services and the explanatory note thereto (A/CN.9/1112, annexes I and II), as well as a compilation of comments submitted by States and relevant international organizations (A/CN.9/1113

[10] *Official Records of the General Assembly, Seventy-first Session, Supplement No. 17* (A/71/17), paras. 235–236.

[11] A/CN.9/1087, para. 11.

[12] Ibid., para. 114.

and A/CN.9/1113/Add.1). It was recalled that the text of the draft model law and the explanatory note as contained in document A/CN.9/1112 did not reflect the further amendments discussed by the Working Group at its sixty-third session (New York, 4–8 April 2022), as summarized in document A/CN.9/1093.

112. As decided by the Commission (see para. 13 above), the Committee of the Whole considered the text of the draft model law and approved the amendments set out below. Provisions of the draft model law not referred to below were approved by the Committee, as contained in document A/CN.9/1112.

B. Consideration of the draft model law and the explanatory note

Article 1

113. With reference to article 1, subparagraph (c), the Committee agreed to retain "electronic identification" as the defined term (A/CN.9/1093, para. 14).

114. The Committee accepted a proposal to amend the definition of "identity management services" in article 1, subparagraph (f), by replacing the word "or" with "and". It was noted that, in order to maintain consistency with the minimum functions elaborated in article 6, it was necessary for the term "identity management services" to comprise services consisting of managing both identity proofing and electronic identification.

115. It was observed that the identity management service provider could also be a "relying party" within the meaning of article 1, subparagraph (j), if the service provider deployed the identity management service for its own purposes (e.g. the identification of its employees). It was added that, in that case, the obligations of the service provider would continue to apply. In response, it was noted that the observation pertained to the explanatory note and did not involve any amendment to the definition of "relying party" in article 1, subparagraph (j).

116. The Committee approved article 1 as contained in document A/CN.9/1112 with the following redraft of subparagraphs (c) and (f):

> "(c) "Electronic identification", in the context of identity management services, means a process used to achieve sufficient assurance in the binding between a person and an identity;"
>
> "(f) "Identity management services" means services consisting of managing identity proofing and electronic identification;".

Article 5

117. The Committee agreed to amend article 5 by inserting the words "the result of" before "electronic identification" in the chapeau (A/CN.9/1093, para. 16).

118. The Committee approved article 5 as contained in document A/CN.9/1112 with the following redraft of the chapeau:

> "Subject to article 2, paragraph 3, the result of electronic identification shall not be denied legal effect, validity, enforceability or admissibility as evidence on the sole ground that:".

Article 6

119. The Committee agreed to amend article 6, subparagraph (d), and article 14, paragraph 1 (c), by replacing "subscribers and third parties" with "subscribers, relying parties and other third parties" (A/CN.9/1093, para. 36).

120. The Committee considered a proposal to add an obligation of identity management service providers to comply with the mandatory law of the place where the service was provided or to which the service was directed. It was explained that the obligation was necessary to ensure respect for mandatory law of the enacting State.

The Committee did not take up the proposal. The Committee also did not take up an invitation to consider including a provision setting out the obligations of the relying party akin to article 11 of the UNCITRAL Model Law on Electronic Signatures.

121. The Committee approved article 6 as contained in document A/CN.9/1112 with the following redraft of subparagraph (d):

> "(d) Make its operational rules, policies and practices easily accessible to subscribers, relying parties and other third parties;".

Article 7

122. The Committee approved article 7 as contained in document A/CN.9/1112 without amendment. A query was raised as to the need for the impact to be "significant".

Article 8

123. The Committee did not take up an invitation to adopt an explicit and more comprehensive approach to the rights of the subscriber.

Article 9

124. The Committee heard of the importance of establishing an appropriate link between article 9 and article 10. As a starting point, the Committee considered a proposal to amend article 9 by inserting the word "reliable" before "method", inserting the words "identity proofing and" before "electronic identification" and inserting the words "in accordance with article 10" at the end of the article (A/CN.9/1093, paras. 18 and 20).

125. It was cautioned that a reference to "reliable method" in article 9 might imply an absolute standard of reliability, whereas there was broad consensus that article 10 established a relative standard of reliability. It was added that the relevant provision in article 10 was paragraph 1, as it established the reliability standard; conversely, paragraphs 2 and 3 set out factors for applying the reliability standard, while paragraphs 4 and 5 did not address the reliability standard per se. Accordingly, it was suggested that article 9 should refer only to article 10, paragraph 1. A preference was also expressed for including the cross reference immediately after the words "reliable method". In response, it was noted that a cross reference to article 10, paragraph 1, alone would only cover reliability assessed ex post. It was therefore proposed that article 9 should also cross-refer to article 10, paragraph 4, which related to services designated ex ante. After discussion, the Committee accepted that compromise proposal.

126. The Committee approved article 9 as redrafted as follows:

> "Subject to article 2, paragraph 3, where the law requires the identification of a person for a particular purpose, or provides consequences for the absence of identification, that requirement is met with respect to identity management services if a reliable method in accordance with article 10, paragraph 1, or article 10, paragraph 4, is used for the identity proofing and electronic identification of the person for that purpose."

Article 10

127. The Committee recalled the differing views expressed in the Working Group on how to deal with article 10, paragraph 1 (b) (A/CN.9/1093, paras. 21–25). The Committee heard a proposal to reformulate article 10, paragraph 1 (b), to provide that the method would be deemed to satisfy the reliability standard if it were proven in fact, by or before a court, to have fulfilled the function described in article 9.

128. Some hesitation was expressed with regard to referring to a court, given that the corresponding provision of the United Nations Convention on the Use of Electronic Communications in International Contracts (2005) (the Electronic Communications

Convention (2005)) did not specify the decision maker. It was also observed that, in some jurisdictions, the decision maker might not be a court. Recalling that article 10, paragraph 1 (b), applied only ex post in the event of a dispute between the parties, it was observed that the body competent to resolve the dispute could also be an arbitral or administrative tribunal. In any event, it was stressed that the body would need to exercise an adjudicative function. The preponderant view was that the model law should specify the decision maker, and that it would be preferable to refer to the "court or competent adjudicative body".

129. A query was also raised about the meaning of facts being proven "by or before a court". In response, it was noted that the words were designed to accommodate different procedures; in one legal system, a court might carry out its own fact-finding, whereas in another legal system, the parties might be responsible for collecting and presenting the facts to the court. Nonetheless, it was accepted that the explanatory note should elaborate on the meaning of the term.

130. The Committee approved article 10, paragraph 1, as contained in document A/CN.9/1112 with the following redraft of subparagraph (b):

> "(b) Deemed to be as reliable as appropriate if proven in fact by or before a court or competent adjudicative body to have fulfilled the function described in article 9, by itself or together with further evidence."

131. The Committee agreed to amend article 10, paragraph 2 (d), by replacing "level of reliability" with the words "level of assurance" and to make the same amendment to article 25 (A/CN.9/1093, para. 32).

132. The Committee approved the remaining provisions of article 10 as contained in document A/CN.9/1112 without amendment. The Committee did not take up a proposal to amend article 10, paragraph 3, by allowing the decision maker to take into account geographical factors if it considered it necessary to do so in a particular case.

Article 14

133. The Committee approved article 14 as contained in document A/CN.9/1112 with the following redraft of paragraph 1 (c) (see para. 119 above):

> "(c) Make its operational rules, policies and practices easily accessible to subscribers, relying parties and other third parties;".

Articles 16 to 21

134. It was proposed that article 16 should be aligned with article 9 by replacing the words "if a method is used" with the words "if a reliable method in accordance with article 22, paragraph 1, or article 22, paragraph 4, is used". The Committee accepted that proposal with respect to articles 16 to 21 and agreed to amend those provisions accordingly.

Article 22

135. It was proposed that article 22, paragraph 1 (b), should be aligned with article 10, paragraph 1 (b), as amended by the Committee (see para. 130 above). In response, it was indicated that, while the formulation of the "safety clause" in article 10, paragraph 1 (b), could depart from the corresponding provision of the Electronic Communications Convention (2005), this was not possible for article 22, paragraph 1 (b), since both article 9, paragraph 3, of the Electronic Communications Convention and article 16 of the draft model law dealt with electronic signatures. It was indicated that a departure from the Electronic Communications Convention could amount to a treaty violation.

136. In response, it was indicated that article 9, paragraph 3, of the Electronic Communications Convention dealt with functional equivalence between handwritten and electronic signatures, which was a matter of compliance with contract law form requirements, while article 16 of the draft model law, relating to a trust service,

provided assurance on data quality, namely, the originator of the data message, and could apply also absent any contract law form requirement. It was also observed that the relationship between the two provisions was one of complementarity and level of detail, and that article 16 of the draft model law could therefore be used to provide additional guidance on how to fulfil the function pursued in article 9, paragraph 3, of the Electronic Communications Convention. It was further indicated that, while consistency with existing UNCITRAL texts should be pursued, ensuring consistency should not come at the expense of legal certainty in the draft provisions or improvements in their drafting, particularly in view of the almost two decades of development in technology and business practices. It was also stressed that the proposed realignment of article 22, paragraph 1 (b), did not purport to modify the Electronic Communications Convention or to constitute an interpretation of its provisions.

137. After discussion, the Committee approved article 22, paragraph 1, as contained in document A/CN.9/1112 with the following redraft of subparagraph (b):

> "(b) Deemed to be as reliable as appropriate if proven in fact by or before a court or competent adjudicative body to have fulfilled the functions described in the article, by itself or together with further evidence."

Article 25

138. The Committee approved the insertion of the words "the result of" at the beginning of article 25, paragraph 1, and the replacement of the word "reliability" with the words "assurance" throughout article 25 (see paras. 117 and 131 above).

139. It was proposed to replace the word "shall" with "may" in article 25 to provide additional flexibility in cross-border recognition. In response, it was noted that article 25 was a core provision to achieve cross-border recognition of identity management services, which was one main goal of the draft model law, and that introducing an element of discretion in the recognition mechanism could undermine legal predictability. The Committee did not take up the proposal.

140. The view was expressed that article 25, paragraph 1, should require the use of a method that offered "at least an equivalent level" of assurance (A/CN.9/1093, para. 29). It was indicated that such an approach would prevent the recognition of identity management services using methods that offered lower levels of assurance than the one used in the enacting jurisdiction. It was added that existing regional definitions of levels of assurance could greatly assist in the determination of equivalence, and that the emergence of global definitions was foreseeable.

141. The view was also expressed that article 25, paragraph 1, should instead require the use of a method that offered "a substantially equivalent or higher level" of assurance. It was indicated that such an approach provided the desired level of flexibility in promoting cross-border recognition of levels of assurance, which was needed in the absence of global definitions of levels of assurance.

142. As a compromise, it was proposed to amend article 25, paragraph 1, by combining the two approaches so as to require the method to offer (a) at least an equivalent level of assurance, if the assurance levels recognized by the enacting jurisdiction and foreign jurisdiction were identical or comparable, and (b) a substantially equivalent or higher level of assurance, in all other cases. A preference was expressed for requiring the recognized levels to be "identical". While some queries were raised about the continued need for paragraphs 2 and 3, broad support was expressed for retaining those provisions with consequential amendments.

143. The Committee approved article 25 as redrafted as follows:

> "1. The result of electronic identification provided outside [*the enacting jurisdiction*] shall have the same legal effect in [*the enacting jurisdiction*] as electronic identification provided in [*the enacting jurisdiction*] if the method

used by the identity management system, identity management service or identity credential, as appropriate, offers:

(a) At least an equivalent level of assurance, where the assurance levels recognized by such jurisdictions are identical; or

(b) Substantially equivalent or higher level of assurance, in all other cases.

"2. For the purposes of determining satisfaction of paragraph 1, regard shall be had to recognized international standards.

"3. An identity management system, identity management service or identity credential shall be presumed to satisfy paragraph 1 if [*the person, organ or authority specified by the enacting jurisdiction pursuant to article 11*] has determined the equivalence, taking into account article 10, paragraph 2."

144. It was explained that, in practice, paragraph 1 (b), of the revised article 25 would be transitional in application, on the basis that, as technical standards were developed and harmonized, there would be greater likelihood for the assurance levels recognized by different jurisdictions to be identical. It was suggested that the explanatory note could be revised to reflect this projection.

Article 26 and title of chapter IV

145. The Committee agreed that article 26 should be amended to align with article 25, and it approved the provision without further amendment. The Committee also agreed to amend the title of chapter IV to read "cross-border recognition".

Explanatory note

146. The Committee considered the proposed amendments to the explanatory note contained in document A/CN.9/1093 (paras. 17, 34 and 36–44) and approved, for the reasons stated in that document, the following changes to the explanatory note set out in annex II to document A/CN.9/1112:

(a) Clarifying the meaning of "third party" in conjunction with the explanation of the term "relying party" in paragraph 89;

(b) Deleting the words "aim to" in paragraph 11;

(c) Adding, at the end of paragraph 68, the words: "under certain conditions. Such limitation of liability should be permitted by the enacting jurisdiction and may not be contrary to its public order legislation.";

(d) Adding, before the final sentence of paragraph 113, the words: "In addition, the obligations under article 6, to the extent that they may apply to the particular identity management system and identity management service provider, may not be derogated by contract.";

(e) Reproducing, in paragraph 148, the definition of "level of assurance" contained in document A/CN.9/WG.IV/WP.157;

(f) Inserting, at the end of paragraph 222, the words: "Since the different functions performed in providing an identity management service (such as those listed in article 6) could be performed in different jurisdictions, article 25 may apply to all or only some of the functions carried out by the identity management service provider, depending on the geographic location where each function is performed.".

147. The Committee also considered and approved the following amendments to the explanatory note:

(a) Inserting paragraph 13 of document A/CN.9/1105 after paragraph 9;

(b) Amending paragraphs 47 and 48 according to the suggestions contained in section 1 of the comments submitted by the World Bank as reproduced in document A/CN.9/1113;

(c) Replacing the first sentence of paragraph 57 along the following lines: "The ex ante approach provides a higher level of clarity and predictability on the legal effect of identity management and trust services thanks to presumptions and reversal of the burden of proof, including when used across borders.";

(d) Inserting the word "ex ante" before "designation" in paragraph 73;

(e) Illustrating possible rights and obligations of a relying party, and their legal basis, in the commentary on the term "relying party", and clarifying that, when the same institution would be both service provider and relying party, rights and obligations associated with each role would apply (see also para. 115 above);

(f) Replacing the word "all" with the word "other" in paragraph 96;

(g) Clarifying, in paragraph 100, that consent inferred from a person's conduct was rebuttable and that circumstances such as the sophistication of the parties and the type of the transaction were relevant considerations when establishing consent;

(h) Inserting, at the end of paragraph 107, the words "without prejudice to the application of mandatory rules.";

(i) Replacing the second sentence in paragraph 111 with the following: "In other words, subparagraph (b) gives equal legal recognition to identity management services that are ex ante designated and to those that are not designated (subject to evaluation ex post), thus ensuring neutrality with respect to the approach chosen to assess reliability.";

(j) Inserting, at the end of paragraph 148, the words: "Nevertheless, such definition of levels of assurance could facilitate international recognition.";

(k) Replacing the words "regardless of the" with the words "at any appropriate" in the last sentence of paragraph 212;

(l) Inserting the word "necessarily" before the word "direct" in paragraph 213.

148. The Committee recommended that the Commission: (a) approve in principle the explanatory note as amended; (b) request the secretariat to finalize the explanatory note by incorporating commentary on the provisions modified during the current session of the Commission; and (c) authorize Working Group IV to review the parts of the explanatory note relating to those provisions at its sixty-fourth session, in 2022. It was noted that, in preparing commentary on the modified provisions, the secretariat could draw on the comments submitted by States and international organizations, to the extent applicable.

C. Adoption of the UNCITRAL Model Law on the Use and Cross-border Recognition of Identity Management and Trust Services

149. After completing its consideration of the text of the draft UNCITRAL model law on the use and cross-border recognition of identity management and trust services and its explanatory note (A/CN.9/1112, annexes I and II), the Commission adopted by consensus the following decision at its 1170th meeting, on 7 July 2022:

"*The United Nations Commission on International Trade Law*,

"*Recalling* General Assembly resolution 2205 (XXI) of 17 December 1966, which established the United Nations Commission on International Trade Law with the purpose of furthering the progressive harmonization and unification of the law of international trade in the interests of all peoples, in particular those of developing countries,

"*Mindful* that the UNCITRAL Model Law on Electronic Transferable Records,[13] the United Nations Convention on the Use of Electronic Communications in International Contracts (2005),[14] the UNCITRAL Model Law on Electronic Signatures (2001)[15] and the UNCITRAL Model Law on Electronic Commerce (1996)[16] are of significant assistance to States in enabling and facilitating electronic commerce in international trade,

"*Mindful also* of the importance of providing a legal foundation for mutual trust to promote confidence in electronic commerce, particularly across borders, and of the increasing relevance of identity management and trust services to that end,

"*Convinced* that legal certainty and commercial predictability in electronic commerce, including across borders, will be enhanced by the harmonization of certain rules on the legal recognition of identity management and trust services on a technologically neutral basis and, when appropriate, according to the functional equivalence approach,

"*Believing* that a UNCITRAL model law on the use and cross-border recognition of identity management and trust services will constitute a useful addition to existing UNCITRAL texts in the area of electronic commerce by significantly assisting States in enhancing their legislation governing the use of identity management and trust services, or in formulating such legislation where none currently exists, particularly with respect to cross-border aspects,

"*Recalling* that, at its forty-ninth session, in 2016, it mandated Working Group IV (Electronic Commerce) to undertake work on the use and cross-border recognition of identity management and trust services,[17]

"*Having* considered, at its fifty-fifth session, in 2022, a draft model law on the use and cross-border recognition of identity management and trust services and an explanatory note thereto, prepared by the Working Group,[18] together with comments on the draft received from Governments and international organizations,[19]

"*Expressing* its appreciation to Working Group IV for its work in developing the draft UNCITRAL model law on the use and cross-border recognition of identity management and trust services and to intergovernmental and invited non-governmental organizations for their support and participation in that work,

"1. *Adopts* the UNCITRAL Model Law on the Use and Cross-border Recognition of Identity Management and Trust Services, as contained in annex II to the report of the United Nations Commission on International Trade Law on the work of its fifty-fifth session;

"2. *Approves* in principle the draft explanatory note to the UNCITRAL Model Law on the Use and Cross-border Recognition of Identity Management and Trust Services, requests the Secretariat to finalize it by reflecting deliberations and decisions at the fifty-fifth session of the Commission, and authorizes Working Group IV (Electronic Commerce), at its sixty-fourth session, in 2022, to review the parts relating to the deliberations and decisions at the fifty-fifth session of the Commission;

---

[13] *Official Records of the General Assembly, Seventy-second Session, Supplement No. 17* (A/72/17), annex I.

[14] General Assembly resolution 60/21, annex.

[15] General Assembly resolution 56/80, annex.

[16] General Assembly resolution 51/162, annex.

[17] *Official Records of the General Assembly, Seventy-first Session, Supplement No. 17* (A/71/17), paras. 235–236.

[18] A/CN.9/1112, annexes I and II.

[19] A/CN.9/1113 and A/CN.9/1113/Add.1.

"3. *Requests* the Secretary-General to publish the UNCITRAL Model Law on the Use and Cross-border Recognition of Identity Management and Trust Services together with an explanatory note, including electronically and in the six official languages of the United Nations, and to disseminate it broadly to Governments and other interested bodies;

"4. *Recommends* that all States give favourable consideration to the UNCITRAL Model Law on the Use and Cross-border Recognition of Identity Management and Trust Services when revising or adopting legislation relevant to identity management and trust services, and invites States that have used the Model Law to advise the Commission accordingly."

VII. Electronic commerce and other legal issues related to the digital economy: progress report of Working Group IV

A. Background

150. The Commission had before it the report of Working Group IV on the work of its sixty-second session (Vienna, 22–26 November 2021) (A/CN.9/1087) and the summary of the Chairperson and the Rapporteur of the work of the Working Group at its sixty-third session (New York, 4–8 April 2022) (A/CN.9/1093). At its sixty-second session, the Working Group had continued its work to prepare the draft model law on the use and cross-border recognition of identity management and trust services, which was before the Commission for finalization and possible adoption at the current session (see chap. VI above). At its sixty-third session, the Working Group had considered intersessional work on the draft model law on the basis of a summary provided by the secretariat. It also held a conceptual discussion on future work on legal issues related to the digital economy, which the Commission proceeded to consider at the present session as part of its work programme.

151. In that regard, the Commission recalled that, at its fifty-first session, in 2018, it had considered a proposal by Czechia to monitor developments relating to the legal aspects of smart contracts and artificial intelligence (A/CN.9/960, annex) and had agreed to request the secretariat to explore the topic, as well as related topics suggested in other UNCITRAL meetings, by compiling information on legal issues related to the digital economy.[20] The Commission also recalled that, at its fifty-fourth session, in 2021, it had: (a) requested the secretariat to continue work on the legal taxonomy of emerging technologies and their applications, which the secretariat was developing incrementally to record its exploratory work on legal issues related to the digital economy;[21] (b) mandated Working Group IV to hold a conceptual discussion on the use of artificial intelligence and automation in contracting with a view to refining the scope and nature of the work to be conducted;[22] and (c) requested the secretariat to continue preparatory work on the topic of data transactions.[23] It also recalled the view, expressed at its fifty-fourth session, that the Commission might eventually refer the topic of data transactions to Working Group IV, to be dealt with in tandem with the topic of the use of artificial intelligence and automation in contracting.[24]

152. The Commission heard that a range of issues related to the scope and nature of work on automated contracting had been discussed during the sixty-third session of the Working Group (see A/CN.9/1093, chap. V). The Commission also heard that the Working Group had set aside time at the session for a preliminary discussion of the

[20] *Official Records of the General Assembly, Seventy-third Session, Supplement No. 17* (A/73/17), para. 253 (b).

[21] Ibid., *Seventy-sixth Session, Supplement No. 17* (A/76/17), paras. 25 (e) and 227.

[22] Ibid., paras. 25 (e) and 236.

[23] Ibid., para. 25 (e).

[24] Ibid., para. 237.

nature and scope of possible future work on data transactions on the basis of the further preparatory work conducted by the secretariat (see A/CN.9/1093, chap. VI).

153. The Commission had before it: (a) a proposal for refining the mandate of the Working Group on the topic of automated contracting (A/CN.9/1116, chap. II); (b) a progress report on the legal taxonomy, and a proposal for a legal guide on issues relating to the operation of distributed ledger systems and the provision of services that leverage distributed ledger technology (A/CN.9/1116, chap. III), as well as a draft new section on distributed ledger systems (A/CN.9/1116, annex); and (c) a note by the Secretariat containing a proposal for future work by the Working Group on data transactions (A/CN.9/1117). The Commission was informed that the deliberations of the Working Group at its sixty-third session had been synthesized and incorporated in the proposals on the topics of automated contracting and data transactions.

B. Guidelines for future work

1. General remarks

154. Broad support was expressed for work to continue in Working Group IV on the topics of automated contracting and data transactions. It was reaffirmed that the work should avoid overlap with the work being carried out within the United Nations system and other international forums, such as work aimed at developing harmonized standards on the ethical use and governance of artificial intelligence, work on data protection and work on cross-border data flows. It was emphasized that future legislative work on electronic commerce needed to foster the broad participation of developing and developed countries and to be complemented by capacity-building activities.

155. It was also reaffirmed that the topics of automated contracting and data transactions were interconnected and interdependent, and that it was therefore appropriate for the Working Group to deal with both topics in tandem. It was observed that future work would need to be organized in a way that was sensitive to the practicalities of considering multiple topics concurrently. One solution put forward was for the Working Group to alternate between topics from one session to the next, which was a working method that had been successfully applied to other UNCITRAL working groups.

2. Automated contracting

156. Broad support was expressed for future work on the topic to proceed incrementally on the basis of a review of business practice and use cases, as indicated at the sixty-third session (A/CN.9/1116, para. 12). The potential for automated contracts to reduce transaction costs and produce economic benefits was emphasized. It was observed that only limited examples of the practical application of automated contracting were provided in the proposal. While a question was raised as to the need for future work to proceed beyond the first stage (i.e. the compiling of existing provisions of UNCITRAL texts that apply to automated contracting), it was acknowledged that new legal issues might emerge as the project progressed, and that the Commission could re-evaluate the direction and scope of the project at each stage.

157. Broad support was also expressed for future work to be guided by the principles of technology neutrality and non-discrimination against the use of electronic means (A/CN.9/1116, para. 9). It was stressed that future work should focus on the application of emerging technologies, not the technologies themselves, and should be carried out in a way that fostered technological innovation.

158. Some support was expressed for proceeding on the basis of a distinction between "automated contracting" and "autonomous contracting" (A/CN.9/1116, para. 6). It was noted that it would be open for the Working Group to consider definitional issues.

159. The Commission accepted the proposal for refining the mandate of the Working Group on the topic of automated contracting and therefore requested the Working Group:

(a) As a first stage, to compile provisions of UNCITRAL texts that apply to automated contracting, and to revise those provisions, as appropriate;

(b) As a second stage, to identify and develop possible new provisions that address a broader range of issues, including those identified by the Working Group at its sixty-third session (A/CN.9/1116, para. 10).

160. The Commission further agreed that, in discharging its mandate, the Working Group should: (a) be guided by the principles of technology neutrality and non-discrimination against the use of electronic means; (b) proceed on the basis of use cases and business needs; and (c) be mindful of the specific needs of developing countries.

3. Data transactions

161. The Commission took note of the distinction between "data provision contracts" and "data processing contracts", as well as the concept of "data rights", as elaborated in document A/CN.9/1117. Broad support was expressed for work to proceed on data provision contracts and data rights as outlined in the proposal (A/CN.9/1117, paras. 56 and 57). Support was also expressed for work to continue on data processing contracts, although it was suggested that, for the time being, such work should be limited to monitoring legislative developments.

162. Several views were expressed with regard to future work. First, it was recalled that work on the topic of data transactions generally should be mindful of intersections with data protection and intellectual property issues. Second, it was emphasized that work should be mindful of the output of other legislative and non-legislative projects, including the Principles for a Data Economy of 2021, jointly developed by the American Law Institute and the European Law Institute, the *World Development Report 2021: Data for Better Lives* of the World Bank and recent legislative projects in the European Union, for example, the "Sale of Goods Directive" and the "Digital Content Directive", of 2019.[25] Third, it was noted that preparatory work on data rights should pay close attention to data rights that might be recognized under existing law, including laws relating to copyright, trade secrets, competition and data protection. A preference was expressed for focusing on data rights in the context of data contracts and not as part of a broader concept of "data ownership".

163. The Commission agreed to mandate the Working Group to proceed with work on data provision contracts on the basis of the preparatory work documented in document A/CN.9/1117. It also requested the secretariat to continue preparatory work on data rights as outlined in that same document, to monitor legislative developments on data processing contracts and, in that regard, to report back to the Commission at a later date.

164. It was acknowledged that no decision was needed for the time being as to the form of the work by the Working Group on data contracts. In that regard, it was recalled that several options had been canvassed at the sixty-third session of the Working Group, including the development of "default" rules to be included in a legislative text, a guide to good practice for parties or a legislative guide (A/CN.9/1117, para. 56).

---

[25] Directive (EU) 2019/771 of the European Parliament and of the Council of 20 May 2019 on certain aspects concerning contracts for the sale of goods, amending Regulation (EU) 2017/2394 and Directive 2009/22/EC, and repealing Directive 1999/44/EC (available at https://eur-lex.europa.eu/legal-content/en/TXT/?uri=CELEX:32019L0771), and Directive (EU) 2019/770 of the European Parliament and of the Council of 20 May 2019 on certain aspects concerning contracts for the supply of digital content and digital services (available at https://eur-lex.europa.eu/legal-content/EN/TXT/?uri=celex%3A32019L0770).

4. Legal taxonomy of emerging technologies and their applications

165. The Commission expressed its satisfaction with the further work done by the secretariat on developing the new section of the legal taxonomy on distributed ledger systems and authorized the secretariat to publish the content of the revised taxonomy in the six official languages of the United Nations. It was noted that, by its nature, the legal taxonomy was a "living document" and that future revisions were anticipated. In particular, the Commission heard that the secretariat would continue to coordinate with the UNIDROIT secretariat with a view to revising the digital assets section of the taxonomy in the light of the outcome of its ongoing project on digital assets and private law (A/CN.9/1107, para. 11).

5. Legal guide on the use of distributed ledger systems

166. It was recalled that the preparation of the new section of the legal taxonomy on distributed ledger systems (see para. 165 above) had identified the need for legal guidance on the operation of distributed ledger systems (described in the taxonomy as the "infrastructure layer") and on contracting for the provision of distributed ledger technology-enabled services (described in the taxonomy as the "application layer").

167. It was added that the proposed guidance document could provide explanations useful to commercial operators, especially MSMEs and operators located in developing countries, in assessing whether distributed ledger technology-enabled services addressed their needs, and the impact of the use of such services on their business. It was explained that raising awareness of those legal issues could promote greater security and sustainability in digital transformation efforts, including within the United Nations system.

168. It was indicated that the guidance document could build on existing UNCITRAL texts and ongoing work at the working group level, as well as the relevant parts of the taxonomy. It was also indicated that the proposed guidance would not take a position on whether particular trade-related activities should be enabled by distributed ledger technology systems (as opposed to other technologies or methods), nor would it mandate specific rules to govern the provision of distributed ledger technology-enabled services or the relations between the parties. It was suggested that it could be presented in an agile format, similar to that of the Notes on the Main Issues of Cloud Computing Contracts.

169. After discussion, the Commission requested the secretariat to prepare a guidance document on legal issues relating to the use of distributed ledger systems in trade, within existing resources, and in cooperation with other concerned organizations, as appropriate.

VIII. Micro-, small and medium-sized enterprises: progress report of Working Group I

170. The Commission recalled the decision taken at its fifty-second session, in 2019, to entrust Working Group I with work aimed at facilitating access to credit for MSMEs, which would draw on the relevant recommendations and guidance contained in the UNCITRAL Model Law on Secured Transactions, as appropriate.[26] It further recalled that such work would strengthen and complete the mandate given to the Working Group by the Commission at its forty-sixth session, in 2013, to work on reducing legal obstacles faced by MSMEs throughout their life cycles, in particular in developing economies.[27]

171. At the present session, the Commission considered with appreciation the reports of the Working Group on its thirty-sixth session (A/CN.9/1084), held in Vienna from

[26] *Official Records of the General Assembly, Seventy-fourth Session, Supplement No. 17* (A/74/17), para. 192 (a).

[27] Ibid., *Sixty-eighth Session, Supplement No. 17* (A/68/17), paras. 316–322.

4 to 8 October 2021, and thirty-seventh session (A/CN.9/1090), held in New York from 9 to 13 May 2022. The Commission was informed that the Working Group, at its thirty-sixth session, had commenced its work on access to credit on the basis of the note by the Secretariat on the subject (A/CN.9/WG.I/WP.124), in which several topics were discussed that could be addressed in a future text on access to credit for MSMEs. The Commission was also informed that the deliberations of the Working Group had resulted in a fully revised note (A/CN.9/WG.I/WP.126) that the Working Group had considered at its thirty-seventh session.

172. The Commission noted that, at both sessions, the Working Group had reviewed the scope and structure of each section of the notes prepared by the Secretariat and that there was general agreement that, in line with the principle of "think small first", the text should mainly focus on micro- and small enterprises, without excluding issues relating to medium-sized enterprises from its scope. The Commission also noted that, although the Working Group had not yet decided on the particular form that the draft text should take, the text would be aimed at assisting States in the adoption or reform of domestic legal frameworks supportive of access to credit for MSMEs.

173. The Commission expressed its satisfaction with the progress made by the Working Group and the support provided by the secretariat. It noted the importance for the Working Group of continuing to deliberate on the topic of access to credit for MSMEs, as opposed to requesting the secretariat to carry out work on the topic with the assistance of a group of experts, as that would allow the reflection of a wider range of perspectives from various geographical regions, legal traditions and countries at different economic levels. After discussion, the Commission thus reaffirmed the mandate of the Working Group in accordance with the decisions taken at its fifty-second session, in 2019.[28]

IX. Dispute settlement: progress report of Working Group II

174. The Commission recalled that, at its fifty-fourth session, it had:

(a) Adopted the UNCITRAL Expedited Arbitration Rules;[29]

(b) Approved in principle the draft explanatory note to the UNCITRAL Expedited Arbitration Rules and authorized Working Group II to finalize the text at its seventy-fourth session;[30]

(c) Requested Working Group II to discuss the topic of early dismissal and preliminary determination and to present the results of its discussions;[31]

(d) Requested the secretariat to hold a colloquium during the seventy-fifth session of Working Group II to explore legal issues related to dispute resolution in the digital economy and identify the scope and nature of possible legislative work;[32]

(e) Decided that some time would be reserved during the colloquium to discuss the desirability and feasibility of work on adjudication.[33]

175. At the current session, the Commission considered the report of Working Group II on the work of its seventy-fourth session (A/CN.9/1085), held in Vienna from 27 September to 1 October 2021, and the report on the colloquium on possible future work on dispute settlement held during the seventy-fifth session of Working Group II (New York, 28 March–1 April) (A/CN.9/1091).

176. After discussion, the Commission expressed its satisfaction with the progress made by Working Group II, in particular its finalization of the explanatory note to the

[28] Ibid., *Seventy-fourth Session, Supplement No. 17* (A/74/17), para. 192 (a).
[29] Ibid., *Seventy-sixth Session, Supplement No. 17* (A/76/17), paras. 189 and 214 (b).
[30] Ibid.
[31] Ibid., paras. 25 (g), 214 (b) and 242.
[32] Ibid., paras. 25 (e), 214 (b) and 233.
[33] Ibid., paras. 25 (g), 214 (b) and 243.

UNCITRAL Expedited Arbitration Rules.[34] The Commission also expressed its appreciation to the secretariat for presenting the legislative options with regard to early dismissal and preliminary determination, based on the deliberations of the Working Group at its seventy-fourth session (see A/CN.9/1114), and for organizing the colloquium on possible future work on dispute settlement.[35]

177. The Commission decided to consider further future work in the area of dispute settlement under agenda item 11 (Work programme of the Commission).

X. Investor-State dispute settlement reform: progress report of Working Group III

178. The Commission recalled that, at its fiftieth session, in 2017, it had entrusted Working Group III with a broad mandate to work on the possible reform of investor-State dispute settlement.[36] The Commission took note of the progress being made by Working Group III in the third phase of its mandate, which was to develop concrete reform elements to be recommended to the Commission. It was noted that progress was being made largely in accordance with the revised workplan prepared by the Working Group at its resumed fortieth session, in May 2021 (A/CN.9/1054, annex). At the same time, the flexibility and the high degree of adaptability of the workplan to the current needs of the Working Group was noted.

179. Taking into account the reports of Working Group III on the work of its forty-first and forty-second sessions (A/CN.9/1086 and A/CN.9/1092, respectively), the Commission commended the Working Group for completing the first reading of the draft code of conduct and for considering the selection and appointment of investor-State dispute settlement tribunal members to a standing multilateral mechanism during those sessions.

180. The Commission noted that progress was being made with regard to other reform elements through a series of intersessional meetings[37] and other informal meetings,[38] as well as by collecting comments on initial drafts of working papers prepared by the secretariat.[39]

181. The Commission expressed its appreciation to the secretariat for closely cooperating with the secretariat of the International Centre for Settlement of Investment Disputes on the code of conduct and with the secretariat of the Organisation for

[34] The publication containing the UNCITRAL Expedited Arbitration Rules and the explanatory note thereto is available at https://uncitral.un.org/en/content/expedited-arbitration-rules.

[35] Further information about the colloquium is available at https://uncitral.un.org/en/disputesettelementcolloquium2022.

[36] *Official Records of the General Assembly, Seventy-second Session, Supplement No. 17* (A/72/17), para. 264.

[37] The fourth intersessional meeting, on procedural rules reform and cross-cutting issues, was held online on 2 and 3 September 2021, hosted by the Republic of Korea (for a summary of the meeting, see document A/CN.9/WG.III/WP.214). The fifth intersessional meeting, on the use of mediation in investor-State dispute settlement, was held in a hybrid format (in person and online) on 28 and 29 October 2021, hosted by Hong Kong, China (for a summary of the meeting, see A/CN.9/WG.III/WP.210).

[38] Informal meetings were held on 26 August 2021, 13 and 14 September 2021, 6–10 December 2021, 20 January 2022, 2 and 3 March 2022, 23 and 24 March 2022, 5 May 2022 and 7–10 June 2022, on the following topics: calculation of damages, the multilateral standing mechanism and its financing, the code of conduct, shareholder claims for reflective loss, the multilateral instrument on investor-State dispute settlement reform, the appellate mechanism, investment mediation, and procedural rules reform. For further information, see the website of Working Group III (https://uncitral.un.org/en/working_groups/3/investor-state), under "Intersessional activities" in the right-hand column.

[39] The initial drafts covered the following topics: third-party funding, the selection and appointment of investor-State dispute settlement tribunal members to a standing multilateral mechanism, the assessment of damages, mediation and other forms of alternative dispute resolution, the appellate mechanism, a compilation of dispute prevention practices, and pertinent elements of selected permanent international courts and tribunals.

Economic Co-operation and Development (OECD) on shareholder claims and reflective loss.

182. The Commission recalled that, at its fifty-fourth session, in 2021, it had decided to recommend to the General Assembly that additional conference resources (an additional one-week session per year) and human resources be allocated to Working Group III for a single period of four years, from 2022 to 2025, on the condition that the Commission would re-evaluate and, if needed, revisit its decision concerning the need for allocating an additional one-week session per year and supporting resources to the Working Group, taking into consideration the Working Group's report on the use of its resources.[40] The Commission was informed that the General Assembly, on 24 December 2021, had decided to allocate an additional one-week session per year to the Commission and the necessary human resources to the secretariat, as recommended by the Commission (see chap. XIX below).[41]

183. The Commission was informed that the additional weeks allocated respectively for 2022 and 2023 had been tentatively scheduled to be utilized in September 2022 (as a two-week session) and in January 2023, both in Vienna (see para. 321 below). While reservations were expressed about the two-week session as limiting the participation of States with limited human resources, it was also mentioned that the two-week session would allow: (a) progress to be made on a number of different reform options in parallel, including the finalization of the code of conduct and the commentary, which should be given priority; and (b) delegations to save costs by avoiding the need to travel twice to the sessions. The Commission was further informed that the secretariat was in the process of recruiting staff members for the three additional posts allocated.

184. The Chair of Working Group III provided an outline of the work to be conducted by the Working Group during the four weeks of session scheduled until the fifty-sixth session of the Commission and indicated that the Working Group would aim to submit the draft code of conduct with the commentary and texts on alternative dispute resolution mechanisms for consideration by the Commission at its next session. While emphasizing the need to take a flexible approach in carrying out the work and the need to adapt the workplan to the current needs of the Working Group, the Commission requested the Working Group to continue its work in an effective manner and urged it to present the outcome of the above-mentioned work to the Commission at its next session in 2023.

185. The Commission took note of the outreach activities of the secretariat aimed at raising awareness about the work of the Working Group and ensuring that the process would remain inclusive and fully transparent.[42]

186. After discussion, the Commission expressed its satisfaction with the progress made by Working Group III and for the support provided by the secretariat on a wide range of aspects, as mentioned above.

187. In addition, the Commission expressed its appreciation for the financial support provided by the Governments of France and Germany, the European Union and the Swiss Agency for Development and Cooperation for travel and simultaneous interpretation, to ensure inclusiveness, and for post-related costs, to enhance the capacities of the secretariat.

XI. Insolvency law: progress report of Working Group V

188. At its fifty-fifth session, the Commission had before it the reports of Working Group V (Insolvency Law) on the work of its fifty-ninth session (Vienna,

[40] *Official Records of the General Assembly, Seventy-sixth Session, Supplement No. 17* (A/76/17), para. 263.
[41] General Assembly resolution 76/229, para. 15.
[42] For example, an event was held in Accra from 24 to 26 May 2022 in cooperation with the International Organization of la Francophonie on different aspects of investor-State dispute settlement reform.

13–17 December 2021) (A/CN.9/1088) and sixtieth session (New York, 18–21 April 2022) (A/CN.9/1094). In addition, the Commission had before it the updates to the publication entitled *UNCITRAL Model Law on Cross-Border Insolvency: the Judicial Perspective* listed in document A/CN.9/WG.V/WP.180 and paragraph 13 of the report of the Working Group on its sixtieth session (A/CN.9/1094), which were transmitted to the Commission by the Working Group for possible approval for publication.

189. The Commission recalled that, at its fifty-fourth session, in 2021, it had adopted the Legislative Recommendations on Insolvency of Micro- and Small Enterprises and requested Working Group V to review and approve the draft commentary to those recommendations at its fifty-ninth session, in December 2021, and to decide whether the approved text should be considered final or should be transmitted for finalization and adoption by the Commission at its fifty-fifth session, in 2022.[43] The Commission noted with appreciation that, in response to that mandate, the Working Group, at its fifty-ninth session, had approved the commentary to the Legislative Recommendations and agreed that the resulting UNCITRAL Legislative Guide on Insolvency Law for Micro- and Small Enterprises should be considered final (A/CN.9/1088, para. 17). The Commission recalled in that context that, at its fifty-fourth session, it had requested the secretariat to publish the final text in dual form, as part five of the UNCITRAL Legislative Guide on Insolvency Law and as part of the UNCITRAL MSMEs texts series.[44] It noted with appreciation the publication of the text in English in both forms and urged the secretariat to issue the publication in other official languages of the United Nations as soon as possible, in the light of the high demand for the text.

190. The Commission also recalled that, at its fifty-fourth session, in 2021, it had referred two new topics to the Working Group: civil asset tracing and recovery, and applicable law in insolvency proceedings.[45] The Commission took note of the progress achieved by the Working Group in the consideration of those topics on the basis of the notes by the Secretariat (A/CN.9/WG.V/WP.175, A/CN.9/WG.V/WP.176, A/CN.9/WG.V/WP.178 and A/CN.9/WG.V/WP.179); reiterated that both topics touched upon a broad range of issues, many of which were complex and required careful consideration; congratulated the Working Group and the secretariat for identifying the key issues involved in both projects and for organizing the work, treating both topics equally; and underscored the importance of close coordination and cooperation in that work with other international organizations, in particular UNIDROIT, whose current work touched upon several issues discussed in the Working Group. Close cooperation and coordination among all concerned was considered important for avoiding inconsistent results, unnecessary duplication of effort and inefficient use of resources. A view was expressed that preparing a separate set of rules on applicable law in insolvency proceedings would be particularly important because of the lack of such rules in many jurisdictions.

191. Finally, the Commission recalled that, at its fifty-third session, in 2020, it had requested the secretariat to prepare and publish an update of the publication entitled *UNCITRAL Model Law on Cross-Border Insolvency: the Judicial Perspective* as soon as practicable, as both a paper and electronic booklet, in the six official languages of the United Nations, using a mechanism along the lines of that used for the 2013 update of the publication.[46] The Commission expressed appreciation to the secretariat for having made updates to that publication available for review by the Working Group at its sixtieth session (those contained in document A/CN.9/WG.V/WP.180) and the additional updates proposed by the secretariat during the session (A/CN.9/1094, para. 13), and to the Working Group for its review and approval of those updates and their transmittal to the Commission for consideration and possible approval for publication. The Commission approved the updates and authorized the secretariat to publish the *UNCITRAL Model Law on Cross-Border Insolvency: the Judicial Perspective* with those

---

[43] *Official Records of the General Assembly, Seventy-sixth Session, Supplement No. 17* (A/76/17), para. 77 (the decision of the Commission, paras. 3 and 4).

[44] Ibid., paras. 74 and 76 (f).

[45] Ibid., para. 217.

[46] Ibid., *Seventy-fifth Session, Supplement No. 17* (A/75/17), part one, para. 63.

updates in the six languages of the United Nations as soon as possible. The Commission stressed that the publication of the updated text in 2022 would be timely, in the light of the twenty-fifth anniversary of the adoption of the UNCITRAL Model Law on Cross-Border Insolvency,[47] on 30 May 2022. The Commission requested the secretariat to keep the publication up to date so that it would continue to fulfil its intended purpose.

XII. Work programme

192. The Commission recalled its agreement to reserve time for discussion of its overall work programme as a separate topic at each session, to facilitate the effective planning of its activities.[48]

193. The Commission took note of the documents prepared to assist its discussions on the topic (A/CN.9/1103 and the documents referred to therein, including the proposals contained in documents A/CN.9/1091, A/CN.9/1101, A/CN.9/1102, A/CN.9/1114, A/CN.9/1116, A/CN.9/1117, A/CN.9/1119, A/CN.9/1120 and A/CN.9/1120/Add.1) and of listed activities of the secretariat planned until the fifty-sixth session of the Commission in support of the legislative work by the Commission and its working groups.

A. Legislative programme under consideration by working groups

194. The Commission took note of the progress of its working groups as reported earlier in the session (see chaps. VII to XI of the present report) and set out in table 1 of document A/CN.9/1103, and agreed on the following allocation of work:

(a) As regards work on MSMEs, the Commission confirmed that Working Group I should continue its consideration of a future text on access to credit for MSMEs that the UNCITRAL secretariat had prepared pursuant to the Commission's request;[49]

(b) With respect to dispute settlement, the Commission agreed that Working Group II should (i) develop a guidance text on early dismissal and preliminary determination as provided in the note by the Secretariat (A/CN.9/1114); and (ii) explore the commonalities that exist in the proposals regarding work on technology-related dispute resolution and adjudication and, in that context, prepare model provisions, clauses, or other forms of legislative or non-legislative text where appropriate;

(c) With respect to investor-State dispute settlement reform, the Commission agreed that Working Group III should continue with its work programme as mandated and encouraged the Working Group to submit to the Commission for consideration at its fifty-sixth session a code of conduct with commentary and texts on alternative dispute resolution mechanisms;

(d) As regards the digital economy, the Commission agreed that Working Group IV should:

(i) As a first stage, compile provisions of UNCITRAL texts that apply to automated contracting and revise those provisions, as appropriate; and

(ii) As a second stage, identify and develop possible new provisions that address a broader range of issues, including those identified by the Working Group at its sixty-third session (A/CN.9/1116, para. 10);

(e) With respect to insolvency, the Commission agreed that Working Group V should continue its consideration of legal issues arising from civil asset tracing and

[47] General Assembly resolution 52/158, annex.

[48] Ibid., *Sixty-eighth Session, Supplement No. 17* (A/68/17), para. 310.

[49] Ibid., *Seventy-fourth Session, Supplement No. 17* (A/74/17), para. 192 (a).

recovery in insolvency proceedings, as well as of the topic of applicable law in insolvency proceedings;

(f) Working Group VI should take up work towards the development of a new instrument on negotiable multimodal transport documents.

B. Additional topics considered at earlier sessions of the Commission

1. Warehouse receipts

195. The Commission recalled that it had decided to place the topic of warehouse receipt financing on its work programme at its forty-ninth session, in 2016.[50] The Commission also recalled that it had considered progress reports by the secretariat at its fifty-first session, in 2018,[51] at its fifty-second session, in 2019,[52] and at its fifty-third session, in 2020, when the Commission endorsed the recommendations set out in the relevant note by the Secretariat (A/CN.9/1014) concerning the scope of the project and the possible content of a model law on the private law aspects of warehouse receipts, as well as the methodology for such work, in particular that it be carried out jointly with UNIDROIT.[53]

196. The Commission also recalled that, at its fifty-fourth session, it had considered a note by the Secretariat summarizing the progress made since the fifty-third session of the Commission by the Working Group on a Model Law on Warehouse Receipts convened by UNIDROIT in consultation with the UNCITRAL secretariat (A/CN.9/1066). The Commission was informed that, at that time, the Working Group had estimated that more than two more sessions would still be needed before it could submit a preliminary draft model law on the private law aspects of warehouse receipts for consideration by the UNIDROIT Governing Council, possibly at the Council's 102nd session, in 2023, and subsequent transmittal to the first available UNCITRAL working group.[54]

197. At the present session, the Commission had before it a note by the Secretariat outlining the progress made by the joint UNIDROIT/UNCITRAL Working Group on a Model Law on Warehouse Receipts since the fifty-fourth session of the Commission (A/CN.9/1102). The Commission took note with appreciation of the progress made by the Working Group and the estimated time for completion of the first phase of the project. The Commission noted the technical difficulty of formulating rules acceptable to different legal systems and the complex issues raised by negotiable instruments and stressed the importance for the working group of adopting technological neutrality and functional equivalence as basic principles for its drafting effort.

2. Negotiable multimodal transport documents

198. The Commission recalled that, at its fifty-second session, in 2019, the Government of China had presented a proposal on possible future work by UNCITRAL towards the development of a negotiable transport document to facilitate the multimodal carriage of goods, particularly by railway in the Euro-Asian space (A/CN.9/998). The Commission also recalled that, at that same session, it had considered with interest the proposal and agreed to request its secretariat to examine the matter further in consultation with other relevant organizations and to report back to the Commission, at its fifty-third session, in 2020, on the progress it had made.[55] The Commission further recalled that, at its fifty-third and fifty-fourth sessions, it had considered the notes by the Secretariat on the results of its exploratory work on the

[50] Ibid., *Seventy-first Session, Supplement No. 17* (A/71/17), para. 125.
[51] Ibid., *Seventy-third Session, Supplement No. 17* (A/73/17), para. 249.
[52] Ibid., *Seventy-fourth Session, Supplement No. 17* (A/74/17), paras. 196 and 221 (b).
[53] Ibid., *Seventy-fifth Session, Supplement No. 17* (A/75/17), part two, paras. 60–61.
[54] Ibid., *Seventy-sixth Session, Supplement No. 17* (A/76/17), para. 220.
[55] Ibid., *Seventy-fourth Session, Supplement No. 17* (A/74/17), paras. 216–218.

topic (A/CN.9/1034 and A/CN.9/1061), confirmed its strong interest for the project, requested the secretariat to report to the Commission, at its fifty-fifth session, on the progress made, including on the preparation of a preliminary draft of a new instrument on negotiable multimodal transport documents, and agreed to give high priority to the project for assignment to the next available working group.[56]

199. At the present session, the Commission had before it a note by the Secretariat summarizing the preparatory work done in response to the Commission's request at its fifty-fourth session (A/CN.9/1101). The Commission was informed, in particular, of the results of the research done by the secretariat and the preparation of a preliminary draft of a new instrument in collaboration with experts and interested organizations, primarily through two expert group meetings on the development of a new international instrument on negotiable multimodal transport documents that were held online on 10 and 11 November 2021, and on 30 and 31 March 2022.

200. The Commission commended the preparatory work carried out by the secretariat since its fifty-fourth session, and there was wide and strong support for assigning work on the development of a new instrument on negotiable multimodal transport documents to a working group for further consideration. Beyond the project on trade and finance facilitation, additional benefits would be the incentive to the digitalization of transport documents, a significant and timely aspect in the aftermath of the COVID-19 pandemic.

201. Noting the various policy questions that needed to be considered by the working group, the Commission agreed that it was not advisable, at the present stage, to limit the mandate of the working group or provide detailed instructions on the approach it should adopt, although it was noted that the deliberations of the working group should avoid interference with existing liability regimes for the international carriage of goods. In that connection, doubt was expressed with respect to the "dual track" approach proposed for the future work, as it was said that the negotiable nature of a transport document was indissociable from carrier liability. In response, it was noted that, while the extent of the carrier liability was an important practical consideration for the holder of a negotiable transport document, from a legal point of view it was possible to deal with the negotiability aspect of transport documents separately from the applicable liability regime.

202. After discussion, the Commission agreed to assign the topic to Working Group VI and requested the secretariat to prepare a preliminary draft text reflecting the outcome of the expert consultations it had conducted since the fifty-fourth session of the Commission and to report back to the Commission, at its fifty-sixth session, in 2023, on the further progress made in the Working Group.

3. Impact of the coronavirus disease (COVID-19) on international trade law

203. The Commission recalled that it had first considered the topic of the impact of COVID-19 on international trade law at its fifty-third session, when it heard a proposal regarding possible future work in connection with measures implemented by States in response to the COVID-19 pandemic. In particular, it had been suggested that the Commission might wish to investigate whether those measures had exposed gaps or obstacles to cross-border trade and investment that could be overcome through work by UNCITRAL in harmonizing cross-border rules (see A/CN.9/1039/Rev.1). After discussion, the Commission had requested the secretariat to explore that proposal further.[57]

204. At its fifty-fourth session, the Commission had again considered the topic (on the basis of documents A/CN.9/1080 and A/CN.9/1081) and requested the secretariat to continue its exploratory work on (a) the issues identified in the progress report as possibly falling within the mandate of UNCITRAL, as well as to continue to hold

[56] Ibid., *Seventy-fifth Session, Supplement No. 17* (A/75/17), part two, paras. 81–82; and ibid., *Seventy-sixth Session, Supplement No. 17* (A/76/17), paras. 223–224.

[57] Ibid., *Seventy-fifth Session, Supplement No. 17* (A/75/17), part two, para. 89.

expert meetings and other events with interested stakeholders to further advance the exploratory work, and (b) the options for establishing an online platform for information exchange by States.[58]

205. At the present session, the Commission had before it a note by the Secretariat setting out further elements relating to the exploratory work regarding, first, issues related to the disruption of the global economy and international trade due to the COVID-19 pandemic, and second, the development of an online platform (A/CN.9/1119). The Commission was also informed that, as part of the preparatory work, a webinar on the topic, entitled "Investor-State dispute settlement (ISDS) stocktaking: pandemic-related measures by States and treaty-based disputes", had been organized in November 2021. A second event, entitled "Crisis impact on international trade law: COVID-19 and beyond – MSMEs and digitalization" had been postponed, possibly to the second half of 2022, in the hope of being able to convene an in-person meeting.

206. With regard to the online platform, the Commission noted that the secretariat had set up a web page containing all of the relevant information related to the project, and heard the suggestion that the secretariat should continue to share such information on the web page. While the proposal to establish an interactive platform was reiterated, it was said that, without additional resources, the secretariat lacked the necessary resources to implement such a project.

207. Regarding the exploratory work, it was said that the impact of the pandemic on international trade law was still significant and that UNCITRAL instruments could support States in developing effective policy and legislative responses and contractual parties in developing contractual responses in the event of unforeseen global crises, to minimize disruption to trade, business and investment, as well as in the recovery efforts thereafter. Support was therefore expressed for the secretariat to continue examining which UNCITRAL texts could be useful to assist MSMEs in a crisis and how UNCITRAL instruments could be utilized to facilitate digital commerce and paperless trade, and thereby reduce trade disruptions and bottlenecks in the event of a future global crisis. It was said that the exploratory work should ultimately result in an emergency kit that could be useful at the outset of any crisis and that would provide information to States, as well as businesses, especially MSMEs, on the effective use of UNCITRAL instruments in case of a crisis. While some support was expressed for that approach, it was also mentioned that the project should not be given priority over other projects.

208. After discussion, the Commission requested the secretariat to continue its exploratory work on the impact of COVID-19 on international trade by holding expert group meetings and other events with interested stakeholders to further advance such work.

4. Climate change mitigation, adaptation and resilience

209. The Commission recalled that, at its fifty-fourth session, in 2021, it had heard a proposal to examine (a) how existing UNCITRAL texts could be aligned with climate change mitigation, adaptation and resilience goals, and (b) whether further work could be done by UNCITRAL to facilitate those goals in the implementation of those texts or through the development of new texts. It was added that public-private partnerships could be an area of focus for taking stock of existing texts, while legal uncertainty regarding the legal status of carbon credits traded in voluntary carbon markets could be a focus for future legislative work.[59]

210. Broad support had been expressed at that time for the Commission to consider the proposal further, on the basis of more precise information on the potential work involved. It was added that member States might need to carry out further internal consultations across different government agencies before a decision on future work

[58] Ibid., *Seventy-sixth Session, Supplement No. 17* (A/76/17), para. 241.

[59] Ibid., para. 244.

could be taken, and that such work would need to be undertaken taking into account existing public international law frameworks, such as the Paris Agreement on climate change[60] of 2015 and the United Nations Framework Convention on Climate Change.[61] After discussion, the Commission requested the secretariat to consult with interested States with a view to developing a more detailed proposal on the topic for consideration by the Commission at its next session, in 2022.[62]

211. At the present session, the Commission had before it a note by the Secretariat summarizing the findings and recommendations of a study on private law aspects of climate change, commissioned from an outside expert with a view to assisting the Commission in considering the desirability and feasibility of undertaking work in that area (A/CN.9/1120 and A/CN.9/1120/Add.1).

212. There was wide agreement within the Commission on the importance of the topic and on the usefulness of exploring how UNCITRAL could offer its own contribution to the international community's efforts to combat climate change and mitigate its effects by updating existing private law instruments and developing new enabling legal mechanisms, if necessary. It was observed that global efforts to combat climate change were an integral part of the agenda of the United Nations. Therefore, as a subsidiary body of the General Assembly, UNCITRAL was well placed to undertake work on those aspects of climate change falling within its mandate, and it would indeed be expected that UNCITRAL would provide its own contribution to support the efforts of other United Nations bodies and Secretariat units in that respect.

213. It was stressed that some regions of the world were likely to be seriously affected by climate change and that developing countries in particular would suffer from its impact and the resulting challenges to their economic and development trajectory. UNCITRAL, it was said, could also play a role in the fight against climate change and that there would be benefits to greater legal certainty in that area. There was strong support for the suggestion that any work to be carried out should be consistent with existing international law and treaties on climate change, where relevant. It was also emphasized that such work should have due regard for the principle of the common but differentiated responsibilities and respective capabilities of States. It was therefore noted that any such work should be guided by the principle of equity, in the light of different national circumstances, and be based upon respect for countries' sovereignty over their natural wealth and resources. Finally, it was said that no measures, including unilateral ones, should constitute a means of arbitrary or unjustifiable discrimination or a disguised restriction on international trade.

214. The views differed, however, as to the scope and focus of such work. The importance of corporate responsibility was highlighted by examples of recent changes in legislation to strengthen obligations on the disclosure of climate-related information, an area in which important standards had been set by the International Sustainability Standards Board, and which should be reflected in any UNCITRAL work. At the same time, however, there were expressions of caution as to the feasibility of work in that area, calling for the Commission not to focus work on tools to facilitate litigation against corporations for climate change-related damages. Instead, it was suggested that focus be placed on private law issues relating to clean investments. In particular with respect to private law issues relating to carbon trading, the Commission's attention was drawn to various international initiatives and regulatory activities that called for close cooperation and a precise delineation of possible UNCITRAL work. The Commission was also informed that the UNIDROIT Governing Council, at its 101st session (Rome 8–10 June 2022) had recommended to the UNIDROIT General Assembly the inclusion of a project to analyse the private law aspects, and determine the legal nature, of voluntary carbon credits in the work programme for the period 2023–2025. The Commission heard expressions of concern

[60] See FCCC/CP/2015/10/Add.1, decision 1/CP.21, annex.

[61] United Nations, *Treaty Series*, vol. 1771, No. 30822.

[62] *Official Records of the General Assembly, Seventy-sixth Session, Supplement No. 17* (A/76/17), para. 246.

about the possible overlap between the proposed UNIDROIT work and its own work in that area. The Commission agreed that any duplication should be avoided and expressed its confidence that all interested organizations would coordinate their respective activities.

215. The Commission also heard several suggestions for improvements to and requests for clarification of the study commissioned by the secretariat (A/CN.9/1120 and A/CN.9/1120/Add.1), which the secretariat was asked to take note of and reflect in any revised version of the study that it might publish in the future. It was also stated that nothing in that study document should be interpreted as implying a change in the rights and obligations of a State party under any existing international agreement.

216. In conclusion, the Commission agreed to request the secretariat to conduct further research in the area, in consultation with outside experts and interested organizations from both within and outside the United Nations system. It also requested the secretariat to organize a colloquium or an expert group meeting on the various legal issues surrounding climate change mitigation, adaptation and resilience, in conjunction with relevant and interested international organizations, the results of which would facilitate its consideration at a future session.

5. Dispute settlement

217. The Commission recalled that, at its fifty-fourth session, in 2021, it had requested the secretariat to organize a colloquium: (a) to explore legal issues related to dispute resolution in the digital economy and identify the scope and nature of possible legislative work; (b) to consider model provisions that could be utilized in the context of technology-related dispute resolution; and (c) to discuss the desirability and feasibility of work on adjudication.[63] It was recalled that those decisions were based on a note by the Secretariat on its activities related to dispute resolution in the digital economy and relevant proposals (A/CN.9/1064/Add.4),[64] as well as a proposal made at the same session that adjudication procedure should be examined with the aim of preparing rules on international adjudication.[65]

218. The Commission further recalled that general support had been expressed at that session that the secretariat should: (a) compile, analyse and share information about developments in dispute resolution in the digital economy; and (b) identify possible means and ways to implement the stocktaking project by utilizing the financial contribution offered by the Government of Japan.[66]

219. The Commission was informed that a colloquium had been held during the seventy-fifth session of Working Group II (New York, 28 March–1 April 2022) to discuss possible future work on dispute settlement (see para. 175 above). The Commission had before it the report on the colloquium, which included a summary of the round-table discussion held on the last day of the session to provide input to the Commission on possible work (A/CN.9/1091).

(a) Dispute resolution in the digital economy

220. With regard to the stocktaking of developments in dispute resolution in the digital economy, the Commission was informed that the Government of Japan, through its Ministry of Justice, had agreed to make a contribution of $368,500 for an initial period of 12 months to implement the stocktaking project. The Commission expressed its gratitude to the Government of Japan for its generous contribution to the project and its willingness to continue to support the project.

221. It was mentioned that the work in that area should be closely coordinated with the work of Working Group IV and that the approach taken by that Working Group in developing a legal taxonomy with regard to emerging technologies and their

63 Ibid., paras. 25 (e), 214 (b), 233 and 243.
64 Ibid., paras. 228–233.
65 Ibid., para. 243.
66 Ibid., paras. 231 and 232.

application could be followed. It was also mentioned that the stocktaking project should focus on ways to preserve the fundamental principles of dispute resolution, including due process and fairness, as well as ways to enhance the efficiency of the proceedings, both of which would build the confidence of the users.

222. Noting the timeliness of the project and the increased use of technology in dispute resolution, the Commission requested the secretariat to continue to implement the stocktaking project on dispute resolution in the digital economy, as outlined in paragraph 29 of document A/CN.9/1091, and to continue to take part in the Inclusive Global Legal Innovation Platform on Online Dispute Resolution, as its experts continued to discuss legal issues relating to online platforms for dispute resolution. The secretariat was requested to report on the preliminary findings to the Commission at its fifty-sixth session, in 2023.

(b) Technology-related dispute resolution and adjudication

223. With regard to the proposals on technology-related dispute resolution and adjudication, there was general support for pursuing legislative work building on the common elements, mainly that both proposals were aimed at providing a legal framework for a simplified mechanism to resolve disputes in a very short time frame involving a third party with the relevant expertise, not necessarily resulting in a final award but the outcome still being enforceable across borders. It was pointed out that the outcome of adjudication, which could be the subject of review in a subsequent arbitration proceeding, was of particular relevance. It was suggested that such legislative work should build on existing UNCITRAL texts, notably the UNCITRAL Expedited Arbitration Rules, which would provide the underlying framework for an expedited procedure.

224. While it was widely felt that there might be merit in tackling the two topics jointly, it was also suggested that such work should build on an analysis of whether it would be desirable to utilize adjudication in a cross-border context and in other industries, including the technology industry, and an assessment of whether it would be feasible to harmonize the legal approaches with regard to technology-related disputes, as well as with regard to the enforcement of the outcome of adjudication. It was generally felt that work should not be limited to the construction or technology industries but rather should address the need to resolve disputes effectively in all types of industry, for example, the financial sector.

225. After discussion, the Commission entrusted Working Group II with considering the topics of technology-related dispute resolution and adjudication jointly, and with considering ways to further accelerate the resolution of disputes by incorporating elements of both proposals. It was agreed that the work should build on the UNCITRAL Expedited Arbitration Rules and that model provisions, clauses, or other forms of legislative or non-legislative text could be prepared on matters such as shorter time frames, the appointment of experts and/or neutrals, confidentiality and the legal nature of the outcome of the proceedings, all of which would allow disputing parties to tailor the proceedings to their needs to further expedite the proceedings. It was stressed that such work should be guided by the needs of the users, take into account innovative solutions, as well as the use of technology, and further extend the use of the UNCITRAL Expedited Arbitration Rules.

(c) Early dismissal and preliminary determination

226. The Commission recalled that, at its fifty-fourth session, it had requested Working Group II to discuss the topic of early dismissal and preliminary determination and to present the results of its discussions to the Commission.[67]

227. The Commission had before it the report of Working Group II on the work of its seventy-fourth session and noted that the secretariat had been requested at that session

[67] *Official Records of the General Assembly, Seventy-sixth Session, Supplement No. 17* (A/76/17), para. 242.

to present the different illustrative options for consideration (A/CN.9/1085, paras. 49–67). Accordingly, the Commission also had before it a note by the Secretariat presenting three legislative options reflecting the deliberations at the seventy-fourth session and inputs from States and other interested stakeholders after the session (A/CN.9/1114) (see para. 176 above).

228. It was generally felt that the topic of early dismissal and preliminary determination was a significant issue in international commercial arbitration. With regard to the legislative options, general support was expressed for developing a guidance text on the topic (option 1) rather than developing a rule for inclusion in the UNCITRAL Arbitration Rules (options 2 and 3). Furthermore, it was noted that Working Group III was in the process of developing a similar rule to enhance the efficiency of investor-State dispute settlement and address frivolous claims. While it was generally felt that the approach to be taken by Working Group III in the context of investor-State dispute settlement would be different, calls were made for the work on the topic to be closely coordinated.

229. After discussion, the Commission entrusted Working Group II with developing a guidance text on early dismissal and preliminary determination, on the basis of the text provided in document A/CN.9/1114, and to present it to the Commission for consideration at its fifty-sixth session, in 2023.

C. Consideration of the role of UNCITRAL in promoting the rule of law at the national and international levels

230. The Commission recalled that it had considered the topic "Role of UNCITRAL in promoting the rule of law at the national and international levels" since 2008. At its fifty-first session, in 2018, the Commission had reviewed the manner in which that topic had been handled within the Commission and had decided to broaden the discussion on the topic to a discussion of the way in which the work of UNCITRAL related to the 2030 Agenda for Sustainable Development and the 17 Sustainable Development Goals.[68] At the same session, however, the Commission had not discussed the desirability for the secretariat to continue holding briefings by the Rule of Law Unit biennially during Commission sessions.

231. At its present session, the Commission considered a short review of its practice in connection with that topic (A/CN.9/1103, paras. 8–10) and proposals by the secretariat to enhance the effectiveness of its consideration by the Commission in future. The Commission recalled the understanding reached at its forty-third session, in 2010, that it was essential to keep a regular dialogue with the Rule of Law Group through the Rule of Law Unit and to keep abreast of progress made in the integration of the work of UNCITRAL into the United Nations joint rule of law activities, as a result of which it requested the secretariat to organize briefings by the Rule of Law Unit biennially, when sessions of the Commission were held in New York.[69]

232. The Commission also recalled that the notes by the Secretariat on the role of UNCITRAL in promoting the rule of law at the national and international levels presented to the Commission at each session since 2019 had already discussed the relevance of texts that were expected to be considered by the Commission at each session to the promotion of the rule of law and the implementation of the Sustainable Development Goals, as well as the expected contribution of the UNCITRAL programme to the promotion of the rule of law and the achievement of the Sustainable Development Goals (see, for example, A/CN.9/1105). Furthermore, the secretariat also provided input every year to the Rule of Law Unit for the annual reports of the Secretary-General on strengthening and coordinating United Nations rule of law activities (see, for example, A/76/235).

[68] Ibid., *Seventy-third Session, Supplement No. 17* (A/73/17), paras. 260–267.
[69] Ibid., *Sixty-fifth Session, Supplement No. 17* (A/65/17), para. 335.

233. Considering the availability of that information, and in the interest of enhancing the efficiency and effectiveness of its sessions, the Commission agreed to discontinue the practice of organizing briefings by the Rule of Law Unit biennially, when Commission sessions were held in New York, noting that the possibility of organizing such a briefing remained, should the need for it arise.

D. Working methods of UNCITRAL

234. The Commission held a discussion on its working methods, in the light of a review of the impact of the COVID-19 pandemic on the ability of the United Nations Secretariat to service intergovernmental meetings, as well as on the availability of delegates and experts for in-person meetings, and the Commission's experience with the adjustments made to its working methods to address those constraints (A/CN.9/1103, paras. 11–26).

235. In the light of the experience accumulated from the holding of UNCITRAL sessions during the COVID-19 pandemic, the Commission considered possible adjustments to its methods of work.

236. While the benefits of discussing and adopting draft reports in person at the final meeting of the working group sessions were highlighted, the Commission decided to allow Working Group III (and any other working group, when the need arose) to use the final meeting of its sessions for substantive deliberations, rather than for the adoption of the session report, and to continue the practice of adopting the report by a written procedure as outlined in paragraph 19 of document A/CN.9/1103. Nonetheless, a concern was expressed about extending a temporary and exceptional measure taken during the COVID-19 pandemic and it was said that the process of adopting the report was an important element of the session, However, the suggestion that the procedure for adopting reports should be consistent among the working groups did not receive support.

237. The Commission further agreed to continue to arrange for the meetings of its working groups to be made available on a streaming or videoconferencing platform, which would allow delegates participating remotely to listen to the deliberations but not make active interventions. It was, however, stressed that any such arrangement should continue to promote inclusivity and should seek to be effective in relation to costs and budgets.

238. In addition, working groups were encouraged to avail themselves of various tools in order to enhance the efficiency and productivity of deliberations during the formal sessions, including by holding informal consultations between or in conjunction with working group sessions. It was observed that such informal consultations could be organized by the secretariat for the sake of transparency and inclusiveness, in order to ensure wide participation. It was also noted that it was necessary to ensure that delegations had equal opportunity to take part in informal consultations. It was emphasized that informal consultations should not be used to take decisions for, or pre-empt or foreclose the decisions by, a working group and that the number of informal consultations should not be excessive, as that could limit the participation of certain delegations.

239. Finally, the Commission requested the secretariat to enhance the tools that it used for collecting and keeping current the contact details of delegates and observers, subject to the required personal data protection measures, in particular by making contact details available to delegates in a closed password-protected system.

XIII. Endorsement of texts of other organizations: the International Standard Demand Guarantee Practice for URDG 758 of the International Chamber of Commerce

240. At the present session, the Commission had before it a note by the Secretariat (A/CN.9/1115) transmitting a request by ICC that the Commission consider endorsing the International Standard Demand Guarantee Practice for URDG 758 (ISDGP)[70] for worldwide use.

241. The Commission recalled its long-standing and fruitful cooperation with ICC, noting that it had already endorsed a number of ICC texts, and recalling, in particular, that it had endorsed the Uniform Rules for Demand Guarantees: 2010 Revision (URDG 758) at its forty-fourth session, in 2011.[71]

242. The Commission further noted that ISDGP was a companion document to URDG 758, as it supplemented URDG 758 by identifying and recording best practice in relation to URDG 758 and beyond. It was added that URDG 758 provided a set of rules applicable to demand guarantees securing monetary and performance obligations in a wide array of international and domestic contracts, and that they were fully compatible with the United Nations Convention on Independent Guarantees and Stand-by Letters of Credit,[72] prepared by the Commission in 1995 and endorsed by the International Chamber of Commerce in 1999.[73]

243. After deliberations, at its 1172nd meeting, on 11 July 2022, the Commission adopted by consensus the following decision:

"*The United Nations Commission on International Trade Law*,

"*Recalling* the general mandate received from the General Assembly, through resolution 2205 (XXI) of 17 December 1966, to further the progressive harmonization and unification of the law of international trade,

"*Recalling* specifically its mandate to coordinate the work of organizations active in this field and to encourage cooperation among them, as well as its mandate to prepare or promote the adoption of new international conventions, model laws and uniform laws and to promote the codification and wider acceptance of international trade terms, provisions, customs and practices, in collaboration, where appropriate, with the organizations operating in this field,

"*Noting* the approval by the Banking Commission of the International Chamber of Commerce, on 31 March 2021, of the International Standard Demand Guarantee Practice for URDG 758, as a companion document to the International Chamber of Commerce Uniform Rules for Demand Guarantees (URDG) 758:

"1. *Congratulates* the International Chamber of Commerce on having made a further valuable contribution to the facilitation of international trade by compiling best practice when applying URDG 758 and offering guidance as to how rules and practices codified in URDG 758 are to be applied regardless of the applicable law;

"2. *Commends* the use of the International Standard Demand Guarantee Practice for URDG 758, as appropriate, in conjunction with URDG 758."

---

[70] Available at https://2go.iccwbo.org/international-standard-demand-guarantee-practice-isdgp-for-urdg-758-config+book_version-eBook/.

[71] *Official Records of the General Assembly, Sixty-sixth Session, Supplement No. 17* (A/66/17), para. 249.

[72] United Nations, *Treaty Series*, vol. 2169, No. 38030.

[73] *Official Records of the General Assembly, Sixty-sixth Session, Supplement No. 17* (A/66/17), para. 248.

XIV. Coordination and cooperation

A. General

244. The Commission had before it a note by the Secretariat (A/CN.9/1107) providing information on the activities of international organizations in the field of international trade law in which the secretariat had participated since the fifty-fourth session of the Commission. The Commission noted the impact of the measures taken around the world to contain the COVID-19 pandemic on the secretariat's efforts in the reporting period to coordinate those activities, some of which had been held remotely by videoconference, while others had been cancelled or postponed.

245. The Commission noted with appreciation the cooperation between the secretariat and UNIDROIT in the preparation of a model law on warehouse receipts (see para. 252 below and A/CN.9/1102). The Commission also took note of the cooperation between the secretariat and UNIDROIT in the area of factoring and, more generally, in the area of secured transactions, as well as on legal issues related to the digital economy (see chap. VII above; see also A/CN.9/1116 and A/CN.9/1117), and further took note of the scope for cooperation with HCCH in connection with legal issues of the digital economy and online dispute resolution (see para. 251 below; see also A/CN.9/1116).

246. The Commission noted with appreciation the coordination between the UNCITRAL secretariat and the World Bank Group on amendments to the World Bank Principles for Effective Insolvency and Creditor/Debtor Regimes relating specifically to the insolvency of micro- and small enterprises, building on the work done in previous meetings of the Insolvency and Creditor/Debtor Rights Task Force of the World Bank Group. The Commission stressed the importance of ensuring coherence between the work of UNCITRAL and that of the World Bank on that matter.

247. The Commission took note of the establishment of the Joint Network for Coordinating and Supporting Secured Transactions Reforms for the purpose of coordinating the activities of participating organizations in providing technical assistance and capacity-building to States and organizations in the area of secured transactions and related reforms. The Network would also aim to coordinate efforts towards international standard-setting in the light of the work of Working Group I (MSMEs) on the same topic. The Commission was informed that the Executive Committee of the Network consisted of representatives of UNCITRAL, the World Bank Group, UNIDROIT, OAS and the Kozolchyk National Law Centre.

248. More generally, the Commission expressed its satisfaction with the efforts made by the secretariat to cooperate and coordinate work with other organizations and entities, within and outside the United Nations system, both at a general level and on specific topics of the Commission's work programme, including the Asian-African Legal Consultative Organization, the Asia-Pacific Economic Cooperation forum, the Energy Charter secretariat, the International Centre for Settlement of Investment Disputes, the Intergovernmental Organisation for International Carriage by Rail, OECD, the International Organization of la Francophonie, OAS, the Organization for Security and Cooperation in Europe, the Permanent Court of Arbitration, the Economic Commission for Europe, UNCTAD, the United Nations Office on Drugs and Crime (UNODC) and WTO. The Commission took note with concern of information on the possible adoption of a model law on public-private partnerships by the Economic Commission for Europe, and the potential duplication of the work undertaken by the Commission on public-private partnerships.[74] In addition, the Commission noted that, at the origin of its work was the decision taken at its thirty-fourth session (Vienna, 25 June–13 July 2001), to formulate core model legislative provisions in the field of privately financed

[74] For example, the *UNCITRAL Model Legislative Provisions on Public-Private Partnerships* (United Nations publication, Sales No. E.20.V.4) and the *UNCITRAL Legislative Guide on Public-Private Partnerships* (United Nations publication, Sales No. E.20.V.2).

infrastructure projects[75] (later expanded to public-private partnerships). That decision, which had remained unchanged in the more recent work, reflected the conviction of the Commission that the diversity of countries' legal traditions and experiences in the area required an instrument adaptable to various sectors and legislative traditions rather than a model law purported to serve all activities and levels of government.

249. The Commission reiterated the importance of coordinating the activities of organizations active in the field of international trade law, which was a core element of the mandate that UNCITRAL had received from the General Assembly,[76] as a means of avoiding duplication of efforts and promoting efficiency, consistency and coherence in the unification and harmonization of international trade law. In that connection, the Commission stressed the importance of closer coordination among the organizations concerned, especially when formulating or considering proposals for future work and when taking up new projects, in order not only to prevent inconsistency but also to avoid unduly burdening their respective secretariats with commitments to participate in and follow up on concurrent projects carried out simultaneously by other organizations.

B. Reports of other international organizations

250. The Commission took note of the statements made on behalf of international and regional organizations invited to the session, which focused on activities of relevance for UNCITRAL.

1. Hague Conference on Private International Law

251. A representative of the secretariat read a statement on behalf of HCCH setting out its continued cooperation with UNCITRAL and noting, in particular:

(a) The cooperation between HCCH, UNIDROIT and UNCITRAL on electronic commerce, insolvency and the judicial sale of ships, as well as the exploratory and preparatory work carried out by UNCITRAL on legal issues arising from the digital economy;

(b) The commitment of HCCH to continue working closely with UNCITRAL and to achieve greater coordination in the areas of work that were reflected on the work programme of both organizations, and to engage in a closer cooperative dialogue in framing their respective work programmes, agendas and timelines, in order to ensure a better deployment of the resources of member States and to ensure harmonization of work undertaken by the respective organizations.

2. UNIDROIT

252. The President of the UNIDROIT Governing Council reported on the developments concerning several UNIDROIT activities. The Commission was informed, in particular, about the following:

(a) At its 101st session, the UNIDROIT Governing Council had made a recommendation to retain the work on the draft model law on warehouse receipts on the UNIDROIT work programme for the period 2020–2022, until the final completion of a first full draft of the model law, expected in 2023, and had also agreed to recommend that the relevant working group draw up a draft guide to enactment, also to be submitted to UNCITRAL after a first draft has been completed, in 2024;

(b) The current UNIDROIT work programme also included other topics of mutual interest, such as the preparation of principles on digital assets and private law, an instrument on the legal structure of agricultural enterprises, a model law on factoring, and the drafting of best practices for effective enforcement. UNIDROIT was fully committed to ensuring consistency between its work on those topics and relevant UNCITRAL instruments, particularly those on secured transactions.

---

[75] *Official Records of the General Assembly, Fifty-sixth session, Supplement No. 17* (A/56/17), para. 369.

[76] See General Assembly resolution 2205 (XXI), sect. II, para. 8.

3. Organization of American States

253. A representative of the secretariat read a statement on behalf of the Secretariat for Legal Affairs of OAS providing the following information:

(a) OAS was pleased to support the Joint Network for Coordinating and Supporting Secured Transactions Reforms (see para. 247 above) and had participated since the beginning of the initiative in 2017. That work was in keeping with the OAS mandate to promote private international law and to do so in collaboration with other international and regional organizations involved in that work. Secured transactions reform was one of the topics specifically identified, because of its importance to equitable access to credit and economic development;

(b) The OAS General Assembly had issued mandates relating to a number of topics in the field of private international law, in particular by way of an over-arching mandate. The OAS General Assembly had instructed the OAS secretariat to promote a greater dissemination of private international law among member States, in collaboration with other organizations and associations, specifically identifying UNCITRAL, among others (HCCH, UNIDROIT and the American Association of Private International Law).

C. International governmental and non-governmental organizations invited to sessions of UNCITRAL and its working groups

254. The Commission recalled that, at its fiftieth session, in 2017, it had requested the Secretariat to provide information about intergovernmental organizations and non-governmental organizations invited to sessions of UNCITRAL in writing for future sessions.[77] At its fifty-fifth session, the Commission had before it a note by the Secretariat submitted pursuant to that request (A/CN.9/1106). The note presented information, as at 17 May 2022, about the newly accepted non-governmental organizations, as well as the non-governmental organizations whose applications had been declined, since the issuance of the last note by the Secretariat on that topic (A/CN.9/1072).

255. The Commission took note of that information, as well as of the separate list of additional non-governmental organizations invited only to the sessions of Working Group III while it was working on issues relating to investor-State dispute settlement reform.

XV. Technical assistance to law reform

A. General

256. The Commission had before it the following notes by the Secretariat, addressing activities undertaken to support the adoption, use and uniform interpretation of UNCITRAL texts ("non-legislative activities"): technical cooperation and assistance activities (A/CN.9/1099); activities undertaken by the UNCITRAL Regional Centre for Asia and the Pacific (A/CN.9/1098 and A/CN.9/1098/Corr.1); and dissemination of information and related activities to support the work of UNCITRAL and the use of its texts, including a report on CLOUT and digests (A/CN.9/1100). The Commission noted that the notes covered activities from 1 April 2021 to 31 March 2022.

257. The Commission recalled that non-legislative activities were designed to harmonize international trade law in practice, and comprised raising awareness and promoting the effective understanding of UNCITRAL texts; providing legislative advice

[77] *Official Records of the General Assembly, Seventy-second Session, Supplement No. 17* (A/72/17), para. 364.

and assistance to States on the adoption and use of those texts; and building capacity to support their effective use, implementation and uniform interpretation.

B. Technical cooperation and assistance activities

1. Report on past activities

258. The Commission expressed its appreciation for the secretariat's work to meet the increased demand for non-legislative activities, noting that, as a result of ongoing COVID-19 measures, most activities had been undertaken online. Some delegations that had hosted online events on UNCITRAL instruments on insolvency stressed the importance of technical assistance activities by the secretariat to raise awareness of and build capacity in the use of UNCITRAL texts. The Commission noted the continuing expansion in the scope and reach of those activities, the focus on beneficiary countries at lower levels of development and the higher participation from Latin America and the Caribbean and from Africa.

259. Noting with interest the further expansion of engagement with academic partners, geared towards young researchers and practitioners in international trade law, including the UNCITRAL Asia-Pacific Days, the UNCITRAL Latin American and Caribbean Days and the forthcoming UNCITRAL Days in Africa, the Commission noted that reports on the UNCITRAL Days observed in 2021 were available on its website.

260. The Commission also heard that the launch event for UNCITRAL Days in Africa, held in Accra on 27 May 2022, had gathered high-level government representatives, as well as representatives of the United Nations Development Programme, the European Union and the International Organization of la Francophonie. In addition, six representatives of the academic community, including five universities from across the continent, had expressed their intention to host an UNCITRAL Days event and discussed the modalities for the events themselves. The Commission welcomed the launch of the series and the commitments of five universities in Africa to host UNCITRAL Days events in autumn 2022, as well as the interest expressed by four additional universities, extended its congratulations and thanks to all participants for their commitment and engagement with that activity and noted that it looked forward to welcoming more universities to join as the events were being organized.

261. In the area of insolvency law, the Commission noted with interest the secretariat's involvement in the multilingual Latin Euromerican G8 Insolvency and Restructuring Program (A/CN.9/1099, para. 43) and the secretariat's plans to promote a further dialogue on insolvency matters across regions and legal traditions. Recalling its calls to the secretariat to intensify its capacity-building activities in support of the judiciary, the Commission expressed appreciation to its secretariat and the World Bank Group for launching the Judicial Capacity-Building Initiative on International Best Practices in the Area of Insolvency Law and welcomed plans to organize the second session in 2023, to be hosted by the World Bank Group. The Commission also noted with appreciation that, in response to its request and the request of its Working Group V, the secretariat had published in January 2022 guidance materials on enacting two or more of the UNCITRAL model laws on insolvency. Noting the twenty-fifth anniversary of the adoption of UNCITRAL Model Law on Cross-Border Insolvency, in 2022, the Commission expressed appreciation to international organizations active in the area of insolvency law for organizing commemorative events, as well as for promoting on those occasions other UNCITRAL insolvency texts.

262. In the area of the international sale of goods, the Commission was informed of the activities undertaken by the UNCITRAL secretariat to celebrate the fortieth anniversary of the adoption of the United Nations Convention on Contracts for the International Sale of Goods,[78] under the name "CISG@40".[79] It heard that the activities had been held

---

[78] United Nations, *Treaty Series*, vol. 1489, No. 25567.

[79] See also *Official Records of the General Assembly, Seventy-fourth Session, Supplement No. 17* (A/74/17), para. 288.

online or in a hybrid format during the COVID-19 pandemic, which had allowed for reaching a broader audience, highlighted trends, including the role of the United Nations Sales Convention in promoting the principles of party autonomy and freedom of contract, and generated ongoing interest among jurisdictions in adopting the United Nations Sales Convention and using it as source for domestic law reform. Finally, the Commission was informed that an informal report on the CISG@40 initiative, including on recent accessions to the United Nations Sales Convention, was available on the UNCITRAL website. The Commission expressed appreciation for the CISG@40 initiative and encouraged the secretariat to continue its awareness-raising activities.

2. Panel on technical assistance activities in the field of insolvency law

263. The Commission commended the secretariat for having held a panel discussion on technical assistance activities in the field of insolvency law at the 1178th meeting of the Commission, on Friday, 15 July. The Commission welcomed the discussion on lessons learned, the perspectives of stakeholders on the available assessment tools and knowledge-sharing and capacity-building platforms, and the role of UNCITRAL legislative, guidance and reference materials and events.

C. Dissemination of information on the work and texts of UNCITRAL

1. General

264. The Commission welcomed the secretariat's outreach activities (A/CN.9/1100, paras. 7–16), including the expanded online and social media presence,[80] and noted with interest that those activities were both generating and meeting increasing interest in UNCITRAL from a broad audience, including those that had not previously engaged with UNCITRAL.

265. The Commission recalled an online programme of learning materials designed to provide an introduction to UNCITRAL, its areas of work and its contribution to the Sustainable Development Goals for government officials, potential UNCITRAL delegates or users of UNCITRAL texts, and the broader public. The Commission also welcomed the issuance of the Chinese-language version of the programme (following the English-language version, launched at the fifty-fourth session of the Commission),[81] and the additional modules to be issued shortly.

266. The Commission noted the important role played by the UNCITRAL Law Library, especially its continued provision of online services and response to information requests during the COVID-19 pandemic, and welcomed the return of normal services at the library.

267. The Commission recalled its request that the secretariat continue to explore the development of new social media features on the UNCITRAL website, as appropriate, noting that the development of such features in accordance with the applicable guidelines had also been welcomed by the General Assembly. In that regard, the Commission noted with approval the continued use and development of the UNCITRAL pages on LinkedIn and Facebook, the Twitter account for the Secretary of UNCITRAL, the Soundcloud account for podcasts, and the increased use of the YouTube account for the dissemination of information on the work and texts of UNCITRAL and use as a point of entry into the Commission's work. For example, during the reporting period, the number of followers of the UNCITRAL YouTube channel increased by 92 per cent and the number of followers on LinkedIn increased from approximately 27,000 to 35,000, a 30 per cent increase.[82]

---

[80] Including the UNCITRAL website (https://uncitral.un.org/) and the presence on Facebook, YouTube, LinkedIn, Twitter and Soundcloud.

[81] *Official Records of the General Assembly, Seventy-sixth Session, Supplement No. 17* (A/76/17), para. 322.

[82] For details on the expanded UNCITRAL social media following, see A/CN.9/1100, paras. 7–10.

268. The Commission noted the important role of the UNCITRAL website (uncitral.un.org) and welcomed the comprehensive statistics on the usage of the website, especially statistics reinforcing the significance of the UNCITRAL website as a multilingual source of information on international trade law. Recalling the General Assembly resolutions commending the website's six-language interface, the Commission requested the secretariat to continue to provide, via the website, UNCITRAL texts, publications and related information, in a timely manner and in the six official languages of the United Nations.

269. The Commission called upon the United Nations Office at Vienna/UNODC Information and Technology Service and the Office of Information and Communications Technology of the Secretariat to provide the secretariat with the necessary technical support to carry out its mandate. Examples of such technical support include implementing a new planning and reporting tool for events and upgrading and incorporating new tools on the website.

2. Forthcoming activities

270. The Commission welcomed the information on activities planned for the coming year, and its benefits as a planning tool for States and other potential participants.

3. International commercial law moot competitions

271. The Commission recalled with appreciation that UNCITRAL co-sponsored a series of international commercial law moot competitions, and that most of the competitions in the period 2021–2022 had been held online. It noted with interest the information provided on the Willem C. Vis International Commercial Arbitration Moot, the Moot Madrid, the Frankfurt Investment Moot, the Spanish-language International Investment Moot, the Foreign Direct Investment International Arbitration Moot, the Second Annual Arabic Moot Competition and the Ian Fletcher International Insolvency Moot.

D. Overall picture of technical assistance to law reform

272. The Commission was highly appreciative of the data and analysis presented, which allowed the reach and impact of non-legislative activities to be better understood. The Commission also welcomed the secretariat's focus on flagship activities, activities with regional and international scope, and activities undertaken in collaboration with States and partners, an approach that was enhancing both efficiency and impact. It welcomed the confirmation by the United Nations Office of Internal Oversight Services that its recommendations of 2019 to enhance those qualities[83] had been implemented.

E. Resources and funding

1. Voluntary contributions to UNCITRAL trust funds

273. The Commission recalled the need for extrabudgetary funds to meet the costs of non-legislative activities and welcomed the secretariat's ongoing efforts to secure additional voluntary contributions to UNCITRAL trust funds (see A/73/17, para. 142, and paras. 274–277 below). Requesting that the secretariat continue those efforts, the Commission recalled its previous statements on the importance of maximizing the benefits from the funds contributed and the need for the secretariat to remain neutral and independent in partnering in the delivery of technical assistance and related activities.[84]

[83] See, further, A/CN.9/1032, para. 72, describing relevant recommendations contained in the report of the Office of Internal Oversight Services on evaluation of the Office of Legal Affairs (E/AC.51/2019/9), at pages 18 and 30.

[84] *Official Records of the General Assembly, Seventy-third Session, Supplement No. 17* (A/73/17), para. 188.

274. The Commission expressed its gratitude to the following States and organizations that had contributed to the UNCITRAL trust fund for symposiums since the Commission's fifty-fourth session (as noted in A/CN.9/1100, para. 79):

(a) To the Government of China for contributions under a memorandum of understanding with the United Nations;

(b) To the Government of France for contributions under a grant agreement to support research on investor-State dispute settlement reform, interpretation and travel;

(c) To the Government of Japan for contributions under a memorandum of understanding with the United Nations in support of stocktaking of developments in dispute resolution in the digital economy.

275. The Commission noted that, despite active fundraising by the secretariat, the balances in the trust funds remained insufficient to meet the anticipated demand for technical assistance activities and requests for travel assistance. The Commission reiterated its call upon all States, international organizations and other interested entities to consider making contributions to the UNCITRAL trust fund for symposiums, if possible in the form of multi-year contributions or as specific-purpose contributions, in order to facilitate planning and enable the secretariat to meet the increasing number of requests for technical cooperation and assistance activities.

276. With respect to the trust fund for granting travel assistance to developing countries members of UNCITRAL, the Commission appealed to the relevant bodies of the United Nations system, organizations, institutions and individuals to make contributions to that trust fund. The Commission also expressed its appreciation to the Government of Austria for its contributions.

277. The Commission recalled with gratitude the ongoing contributions and support from the European Commission, the Organization of the Petroleum Exporting Countries (OPEC) Fund for International Development and the Federal Ministry for Economic Cooperation and Development of Germany for the Transparency Registry and for promoting the UNCITRAL transparency standards.

2. Internship programme

278. The Commission welcomed the continuation of the internship programme in both the UNCITRAL secretariat in Vienna and in the Regional Centre, and the resumption of some in-person internships. It also welcomed the fact that remote internships had reduced underrepresentation from some regional groups and had enhanced linguistic and geographical diversity, and, with a view to continuing that encouraging trend, requested States and observer organizations to bring the possibility of an internship at UNCITRAL to the attention of interested persons and to consider granting scholarships for the purpose of attracting those most qualified for an internship at UNCITRAL.

F. UNCITRAL presence in the Asia-Pacific region

279. The Commission had before it a note by the Secretariat on the activities undertaken by its Regional Centre for Asia and the Pacific in the period since the last report to the Commission, in 2021 (A/CN.9/1098 and A/CN.9/1098/Corr.1).

280. The Commission recognized benefits in the region resulting from the regional activities of the secretariat, through its Regional Centre, in the levels of awareness, adoption and implementation of harmonized and modern international trade law standards elaborated by UNCITRAL. Examples included the accession by Iraq to the Convention on the Recognition and Enforcement of Foreign Arbitral Awards (New York, 1958)[85] and the United Nations Convention on Transparency in Treaty-based Investor-State Arbitration (New York, 2014),[86] and the signature of Australia to and

[85] United Nations, *Treaty Series*, vol. 330, No. 4739.

[86] General Assembly resolution 69/116, annex.

ratification by Georgia and Türkiye of the Singapore Convention on Mediation. (For other treaty actions and enactments, see also chap. XVII below.) In addition, the Regional Centre provided technical assistance and capacity-building to four landlocked developing countries (the Lao People's Democratic Republic, Mongolia, Nepal and Turkmenistan). The Commission also highlighted the impact of the Regional Centre in mobilizing contributions to the work of UNCITRAL from the Asia-Pacific region, noting that the activities carried out during the reporting period had resulted in broader and deeper stakeholder engagement in the region and beyond.

281. The Commission noted that the Regional Centre was staffed with one professional-level staff member, one programme assistant, one team assistant and two legal expert secondees, and that its core project budget allowed for the occasional employment of experts and consultants. During the reporting period, the Regional Centre had received 21 interns. The Commission also noted that the Regional Centre relied fully on the annual financial contribution from the Incheon Metropolitan City to the UNCITRAL trust fund for symposiums to meet the costs of its operation and programme ($500,000 from 2011 to 2016 and $450,000 from 2017 to 2026). The Commission expressed its gratitude to the Incheon Metropolitan City, and further expressed its gratitude to the Ministry of Justice of the Republic of Korea and to the government of Hong Kong, China, for the extension of their contribution of two legal experts on non-reimbursable loans.

282. The Commission commended the Regional Centre for having continued to deliver flagship activities despite continued complications arising from the COVID-19 pandemic during the reporting period, namely, the second edition of the Incheon Law and Business Forum (Incheon, Republic of Korea, 6 and 7 September 2021), the fourth edition of the UNCITRAL Asia Pacific Judicial Summit (Hong Kong, China, 1 and 2 November 2021), the tenth edition of the Asia-Pacific Alternative Dispute Resolution Conference, including the UNCITRAL special session (Seoul, 2–5 November 2021), and the eighth edition of the UNCITRAL Asia-Pacific Day. Regarding the latter, the Commission welcomed the ground-breaking total of 21 events co-hosted with various universities across 14 jurisdictions in the region during the last quarter of 2021, which, as in previous years, had proved highly successful in supporting the activities and objectives of the Regional Centre, and in the current year had expanded the flagship series to Maldives, Nepal, Sri Lanka and Turkmenistan for the first time.[87]

283. The Commission noted with appreciation the additional events and public, private and civil society initiatives that the Regional Centre had organized or supported through participation of the secretariat, and the technical assistance and capacity-building services provided to States, international and regional organizations and development banks in the region. The Commission welcomed the statement by the delegation of the Republic of Korea congratulating the Regional Centre on its tenth anniversary and confirming the continuation of its support for the Regional Centre in promoting legal certainty in international commercial transactions in Asia and the Pacific.

284. It also expressed strong support for the Regional Centre's continued coordination and cooperation efforts with regional stakeholders, development banks and other institutions active in trade law reform, as well as with United Nations funds, programmes and specialized agencies active in the region.

285. The Commission encouraged the secretariat to continue to seek cooperation, including through formal agreements, to ensure coordination and funding for the technical assistance and capacity-building activities of the Regional Centre. It repeated its call upon all States, international organizations and other interested entities to consider making contributions to UNCITRAL trust funds to enable the continued delivery of those activities.

[87] For further information, see the "UNCITRAL Asia-Pacific Day report 2021", available at https://uncitral.un.org/sites/uncitral.un.org/files/media-documents/uncitral/en/apdayreport_2021.pdf.

XVI. Promotion of ways and means of ensuring a uniform interpretation and application of UNCITRAL legal texts

286. The Commission recalled the importance of the CLOUT system, including the digests of case law, in promoting the uniform interpretation of those texts. It welcomed the information on the issues of CLOUT published in the period 2021–2022, the 70 cases reported in the period 2021–2022 and the information on the pattern of contributions to, and use of, the CLOUT system (A/CN.9/1100, paras. 17–20).

287. The Commission noted with interest the progress made in the effort towards a rejuvenation of the CLOUT system, and the effort's focus on building a more active and productive network of CLOUT contributors and covering an expanded range of UNCITRAL texts.

288. With regard to building a more active and productive network of CLOUT contributors, the Commission requested the secretariat to continue the approach set out in document A/CN.9/1100, paras. 26 to 29. The Commission reiterated its previous calls for contributions from all legal traditions to its uniform interpretation tools, including from voluntary contributors, institutional partners and national correspondents. It commended the secretariat's proposals to establish a CLOUT community of contributors comprising national correspondents, partners and voluntary contributors, to be called the "CLOUT Network", and to organize regular meetings of the Network in conjunction with technical assistance activities of the secretariat, such as the UNCITRAL Days in various regions and/or the Willem C. Vis International Commercial Arbitration Moot in Vienna.

289. The Commission expressed its thanks to States, organizations, institutions and individuals that had contributed to the CLOUT system, whether as individual or institutional contributors, and appealed to all States and stakeholders to become active contributors to the CLOUT Network. The Commission also requested the secretariat to develop tools that would formally recognize those contributions, such as those set out in document A/CN.9/1100, paragraph 29 (d).

290. The Commission welcomed the nomination of more than 70 national correspondents from States that had enacted UNCITRAL texts, and recalled its agreement to the establishment of a Steering Committee for CLOUT, comprising one representative appointed by each State.[88] In that regard, the Commission noted that a Steering Committee would be selected from among those nominated as national correspondents, and: (a) highlighted the importance of representation from all regional groups, from different legal traditions and from individuals with expertise across UNCITRAL subject areas; (b) requested that the Chair of UNCITRAL and serving or recently serving Chairs of its working groups be ex officio members of the Steering Committee; and (c) expressed the wish that representatives should be drawn from States that had ratified uniform UNCITRAL texts. The Commission also noted that representatives to the Steering Committee should be appointed for a period of five years, as was the case for national correspondents.

291. The Commission noted that the role of the Steering Committee would be to provide support and encouragement to the CLOUT Network, through such activities as reporting on case law databases and sources of information relevant to the CLOUT system, raising awareness of the CLOUT system in all regions, monitoring the pattern of CLOUT contributions, making recommendations towards ensuring that CLOUT cases reflected the adoption and use of UNCITRAL texts in different legal systems and across all regions, and encouraging an expanded scope of UNCITRAL texts covered. The Commission welcomed the proposal that the Steering Committee would meet once per year, in conjunction with the Willem C. Vis International Commercial Arbitration Moot, to consider progress on those matters made over the preceding year.

[88] *Official Records of the General Assembly, Seventy-fourth Session, Supplement No. 17* (A/74/17), paras. 239–244.

292. As regards a further goal, a sustainable solution to the electronic dissemination of CLOUT, the Commission requested the secretariat to modernize the design and format of CLOUT issues for an eventual migration to a new, upgraded platform and a searchable format, which would ensure that searches for CLOUT abstracts and digests would generate individual abstracts and relevant returns from within the digests. Noting that that upgrade would involve budgetary implications, the Commission called upon the United Nations Secretariat to provide the information and communications technology resources that would be needed for such a migration.

293. In the case that such resources were not made available, the Commission also called upon States, organizations, institutions and individuals to consider further supporting the sustainable electronic dissemination of CLOUT through contributions to UNCITRAL trust funds for that purpose.

294. The Commission took note with satisfaction of the performance of the 1958 New York Convention Guide website[89] and the successful coordination between that website and the CLOUT system.

XVII. Status of conventions and model laws and the operation of the Transparency Registry

A. General discussion

295. The Commission considered the status of the conventions and model laws emanating from its work and the status of the 1958 New York Convention, on the basis of a note by the Secretariat (A/CN.9/1097). The Commission noted with appreciation the information on treaty actions and legislative enactments received since its fifty-fourth session.

296. On the occasion of the "UNCITRAL Digital Trade Week", on 7 July 2022, the Philippines deposited its instrument of ratification of the Electronic Communications Convention (2005).[90] During the ceremony of deposit, it was explained that the ratification was a significant milestone in strengthening cross-border international trade with key trading partners of the Philippines, some of which were already parties to the Convention, as it ensured that fundamental principles of e-commerce law were recognized and enforced across borders. It was also indicated that the adoption of the Convention was in line with a number of free trade agreements to which the Philippines was a party, and that it could assist in realizing the benefits expected from those trade agreements, as well as support paperless trade facilitation

297. The Commission also noted the following actions and legislative enactments made known to the UNCITRAL secretariat subsequent to the submission of the above-mentioned note:

(a) United Nations Convention on Contracts for the International Sale of Goods (Vienna, 1980), as amended by the Protocol of 11 April 1980 (Vienna): accession by Turkmenistan (2022) and deposit of declaration of territorial application to Hong Kong SAR by China (2022) (95 States parties);

(b) United Nations Convention on International Settlement Agreements Resulting from Mediation (New York, 2018): ratification by Kazakhstan (2022) (10 States parties);

(c) United Nations Convention on the Use of Electronic Communications in International Contracts (New York, 2005):[91] new action by the Philippines (ratification) (16 States Parties); domestic legislation enacting the substantive

---

[89] Available at www.newyorkconvention1958.org.

[90] General Assembly resolution 60/21, annex.

[91] Ibid.

provisions of the Convention has been adopted in 40 States; new domestic legislation based on the Convention has been adopted in Maldives (2022);

(d) UNCITRAL Model Law on Electronic Commerce (1996): legislation based on or influenced by the Model Law has been adopted in 82 States in a total of 162 jurisdictions; new Legislation based on the Model Law has been adopted in Maldives (2022) and Eswatini (2022);

(e) UNCITRAL Model Law on Electronic Signatures (2001): legislation based on or influenced by the Model Law has been adopted in 38 States; new legislation based on the Model Law has been adopted in Maldives (2022).

298. The Commission expressed appreciation to the General Assembly for the support it provided to UNCITRAL in its activities and in performing its distinct role in furthering the dissemination of international commercial law. In particular, the Commission referred to the long-established practice of the General Assembly, upon acting on UNCITRAL texts, of recommending to States to give favourable consideration to UNCITRAL texts and requesting the Secretary-General to publish UNCITRAL texts, including electronically, in the six official languages of the United Nations, and taking other measures to disseminate UNCITRAL texts as broadly as possible to Governments and all other relevant stakeholders.

B. Operation of the Transparency Registry

299. The Commission recalled that the repository of published information under the UNCITRAL Rules on Transparency in Treaty-based Investor-State Arbitration, adopted at its forty-sixth session in 2013 (the "Transparency Registry"), had been established under article 8 of the Rules on Transparency. The Commission also recalled the request by the General Assembly to the Secretary-General to continue the operation of the Transparency Registry, through the secretariat of the Commission and funded entirely by voluntary contributions until the end of 2023, and to keep the General Assembly informed of developments.[92]

300. The Commission further recalled the note by the Secretariat on the status of conventions and model laws and the operation of the Transparency Registry, which provided an update on the Rules on Transparency and the Transparency Registry (A/CN.9/1097, paras. 16–18).

301. The Commission expressed its appreciation to the Federal Ministry for Economic Cooperation and Development of Germany, the European Commission and the OPEC Fund for International Development for their voluntary contributions to support the Transparency Registry. The Commission also expressed its appreciation to the European Commission for its renewed commitment to providing funding for the Registry through 2023, which would allow the UNCITRAL secretariat to continue operating the Registry, as well as for promoting the UNCITRAL transparency standards.

C. Bibliography of recent writings related to the work of UNCITRAL

302. The Commission recalled that the UNCITRAL Law Library specialized in international commercial law. The Library's collection featured important titles and online resources in that field in the six United Nations official languages. From 1 April 2021 to 31 March 2022, library staff had responded to approximately 339 reference requests, originating from 59 countries. Measures introduced as a result of the COVID-19 pandemic meant that there had been few visitors to the UNCITRAL Law Library.

303. Considering the broader impact of UNCITRAL texts, the Commission took note of the bibliography of recent writings related to the work of UNCITRAL (A/CN.9/1096) and the influence of UNCITRAL texts as described in academic and professional

[92] General Assembly resolution 75/133, paras. 4 and 5.

literature. The Commission noted in particular that the consolidated bibliography contained more than 11,702 entries, reproduced in English and in the original language. The Commission also noted the importance of facilitating a comprehensive approach to the creation of the bibliography and the need to remain informed of the activities of non-governmental organizations active in the field of international trade law. In that regard, the Commission recalled and repeated its request that non-governmental organizations invited to the annual sessions of the Commission donate copies of their journals, reports and other publications to the UNCITRAL Law Library for review.[93] The Commission expressed appreciation to all non-governmental organizations that had donated materials.

XVIII. Current role of UNCITRAL in promoting the rule of law

A. Introduction

304. The Commission recalled that the item on the current role of UNCITRAL in promoting the rule of law had been on the agenda of the Commission since its forty-first session, in 2008,[94] in response to the General Assembly's invitation to the Commission to comment, in its report to the General Assembly, on the Commission's current role in promoting the rule of law.[95] The Commission further recalled that, at its forty-first to fifty-fourth sessions, in 2008 to 2021, respectively, the Commission, in its annual reports to the General Assembly,[96] had transmitted comments on its role in promoting the rule of law at the national and international levels.

305. At the current session, the Commission had before it a note by the Secretariat on the role of UNCITRAL in promoting the rule of law at the national and international levels (A/CN.9/1105). The Commission noted that the General Assembly, in its resolution 76/117, had reiterated its invitation to the Commission to comment on its current role in promoting the rule of law. The Commission noted that the same resolution indicated that the upcoming debates of the Sixth Committee under the agenda item on the rule of law would focus on the subtopic "The impacts of the global coronavirus disease (COVID-19) pandemic on the rule of law at the national and international levels".[97] (For comments of the Commission transmitted to the General Assembly under this agenda item, as requested in para. 20 of General Assembly resolution 76/117, see sect. B below.)

306. The Commission highlighted the relevance of its work to the promotion of the rule of law and the implementation of the Sustainable Development Goals. The Commission took note of the invitation by the secretariat to consider whether the criteria it used for

---

[93] *Official Records of the General Assembly, Seventieth Session, Supplement No. 17* (A/70/17), para. 264.

[94] For the decision of the Commission to include the item on its agenda, see *Official Records of the General Assembly, Sixty-second Session, Supplement No. 17* (A/62/17), part two, paras. 111–113.

[95] General Assembly resolutions 62/70, para. 3; 63/128, para. 7; 64/116, para. 9; 65/32, para. 10; 66/102, para. 12; 67/97, para. 14; 68/116, para. 14; 69/123, para. 17; 70/118, para. 20; 71/148, para. 22; 72/119, para. 25; 73/207, para. 20; 74/191, para. 20; 75/141, para. 20; and 76/117, para. 20.

[96] *Official Records of the General Assembly, Sixty-third Session, Supplement No. 17* and corrigendum (A/63/17 and A/63/17/Corr.1), para. 386; ibid., *Sixty-fourth Session, Supplement No. 17* (A/64/17), paras. 413–419; ibid., *Sixty-fifth Session, Supplement No. 17* (A/65/17), paras. 313–336; ibid., *Sixty-sixth Session, Supplement No. 17* (A/66/17), paras. 299–321; ibid., *Sixty-seventh Session, Supplement No. 17* (A/67/17), paras. 195–227; ibid., *Sixty-eighth Session, Supplement No. 17* (A/68/17), paras. 267–291; ibid., *Sixty-ninth Session, Supplement No. 17* (A/69/17), paras. 215–240; ibid., *Seventieth Session, Supplement No. 17* (A/70/17), paras. 318–324; ibid., *Seventy-first Session, Supplement No. 17* (A/71/17), paras. 317–342; ibid., *Seventy-second Session, Supplement No. 17* (A/72/17), paras. 435–441; ibid., *Seventy-third Session, Supplement No. 17* (A/73/17), paras. 232–233; ibid., *Seventy-fourth Session, Supplement No. 17* (A/74/17), paras. 303–308; *Seventy-fifth Session, Supplement No. 17* (A/75/17), part one, para. 25; and ibid., *Seventy-sixth Session, Supplement No. 17* (A/76/17), paras. 370–374.

[97] General Assembly resolution 76/117, para. 23.

assessing the feasibility and desirability of undertaking work on a new topic[98] could be applied to ensure even greater alignment of its work with the Sustainable Development Goals, considering that the Goals were time-bound (until 2030).

307. The Commission reiterated its request to States, the secretariat, organizations and institutions to continue their efforts towards increasing awareness of the role of UNCITRAL standards and activities for the promotion of the rule of law at the national and international levels and of their contribution to the implementation of the Sustainable Development Goals. In that context, the Commission noted that the high-level political forum on sustainable development, which usually took place in parallel with annual sessions of UNCITRAL, provided an annual opportunity for States, the secretariat, organizations and institutions to highlight the role of UNCITRAL in the implementation of the Sustainable Development Goals.[99]

B. UNCITRAL comments to the General Assembly

308. In formulating its comments to the General Assembly in response to the invitation contained in paragraph 23 of General Assembly resolution 76/117, the Commission bore in mind the subtopic of the upcoming debates of the Sixth Committee on the rule of law, "The impacts of the global coronavirus disease (COVID-19) pandemic on the rule of law at the national and international levels". The comments provided a review of the discussion of the subtopic at prior sessions, described relevant exploratory work and outlined the relevance of texts to the subtopic in the areas of electronic commerce, MSMEs, insolvency, the international sale of goods, public-private partnerships and public procurement, mediation, arbitration and secured transactions.

309. The Commission recalled its consideration of issues relevant to that subtopic at its sessions in 2020[100] and 2021.[101] In 2020, the Commission requested the secretariat to organize a series of virtual panels to consider the important role the tools that UNCITRAL has developed can play in the COVID-19 response and recovery efforts of States.[102] In 2021, the Commission hosted a series of events to support States in commercial law reform and to highlight the importance of resilience in that framework to facilitate COVID-19 economic recovery.[103]

310. The Commission noted its request to the secretariat to conduct exploratory work to identify and address gaps or obstacles in the international commercial law framework that had been exposed by the COVID-19 pandemic.[104] At the request of the Commission, the secretariat circulated a questionnaire asking States to share their best practices and experiences in responding to the impact of COVID-19 on international trade.[105] The results of the responses were summarized in document A/CN.9/1080. The secretariat also held webinars on the topics of the digitalization of international trade, a simplified insolvency regime for micro- and small enterprises, and COVID-19 measures implemented by States. That work had led to a more comprehensive understanding of the impact that COVID-19 has had on cross-border trade and its legal framework, while

---

[98] *Official Records of the General Assembly, Sixty-eighth Session, Supplement No. 17* (A/68/17), paras. 294–295.

[99] For example, the theme of the Forum held from 5 to 7 July and from 11 to 15 July 2022 was "Building back better from the coronavirus disease (COVID-19) while advancing the full implementation of the 2030 Agenda for Sustainable Development", with a focus on Sustainable Development Goals 4 on quality education, 5 on gender equality, 14 on life below water, 15 on life on land, and 17 on partnerships for the Goals, and will consider the impacts of the COVID-19 pandemic across the Sustainable Development Goals.

[100] *Official Records of the General Assembly, Seventy-fifth Session, Supplement No. 17* (A/75/17), part one, paras. 107–117.

[101] Ibid., *Seventy-sixth Session, Supplement No. 17* (A/76/17) paras. 238–241.

[102] Further information on the panels is available at https://uncitral.un.org/en/COVID-19-panels.

[103] Further information on the side events is available at https://uncitral.un.org/en/content/side-events-54th-commission-session.

[104] *Official Records of the General Assembly, Seventy-fifth Session, Supplement No. 17* (A/75/17), part two, para. 89.

[105] Ibid., *Seventy-sixth Session, Supplement No. 17* (A/76/17) para. 239.

providing detailed information about the legal responses implemented by States to address the impact of COVID-19.

311. The Commission also noted that the subtopic was relevant to the Commission's work in all its subject areas, but particularly relevant to texts in the areas of electronic commerce, MSMEs, insolvency, the international sale of goods, public-private partnerships and public procurement, mediation, arbitration and secured transactions.

312. The Commission highlighted the positive role played by the following UNCITRAL texts during the COVID-19 pandemic:

(a) In the area of electronic commerce, the importance of the UNCITRAL Model Law on Electronic Transferable Records had been noted for its role in supporting supply chains, especially for MSMEs, which had been particularly negatively affected by liquidity shortages and difficulties in accessing credit;

(b) In the area of MSMEs and insolvency, both the UNCITRAL Legislative Recommendations on Insolvency of Micro- and Small Enterprises and the UNCITRAL Legislative Recommendations on Limited Liability Enterprises were recognized as tools that could help mitigate the effects of the measures required to control the pandemic. Many businesses, especially MSMEs, became insolvent or were still expected to become insolvent due to the COVID-19 crisis. The UNCITRAL Legislative Recommendations on Insolvency of Micro- and Small Enterprises provided micro- and small enterprises with a simplified, equitable, fast, flexible and cost-efficient manner of resolving insolvency issues and could help deserving micro- and small enterprises to restart entrepreneurial activities, thereby preserving jobs and other positive economic activity. The UNCITRAL Legislative Recommendations on Limited Liability Enterprises provided a legal form that enabled entrepreneurs to protect personal assets if their businesses became distressed or insolvent;

(c) In the area of international sale of goods, article 79 of the United Nations Sales Convention, provided an exemption from liability if a party could prove that its failure to perform obligations was due to an impediment beyond its control and that it could not reasonably be expected to have taken the impediment into account at the time of the conclusion of the contract or to have avoided or overcome it, or its consequences;

(d) In the area of public-private partnerships and public procurement, the COVID-19 pandemic had affected public-private partnership contracts and it was necessary to have an adaptation mechanism between the contracting authority and the private partner to address cost increases in the provision of public services or unexpected financial changes. The mechanism for contract adaptation in the *UNCITRAL Model Legislative Provisions on Public-Private Partnerships*[106] was recognized as being relevant to that context;

(e) In the area of mediation, the UNCITRAL mediation framework provided a suite of texts that supported mediation, from its initiation through to the enforcement of the settlement agreement under the Singapore Convention on Mediation. That framework might be particularly suitable for MSMEs, which might not have the financial resources or the time to pursue solutions through adversarial dispute settlement, and would thus increase access to justice. Especially in the post-pandemic recovery phase, flexible, cost- and time-efficient methods of dispute resolution would be particularly important to overcome the consequences of the crisis and enable parties to find solutions to conflicts;

(f) In the area of arbitration, the COVID-19 pandemic had required arbitral institutions to take measures to respond to the crisis, ranging from measures to ensure the safe operation of the institutions to measures aimed at the effective administration of arbitral proceedings. During the pandemic, the number of expedited arbitration proceedings increased and there was an increased use of digitization and technology in arbitration proceedings. These trends were expected to continue in the post-pandemic environment. The UNCITRAL texts on dispute resolution were flexible enough to

[106] United Nations publication, Sales No. E.20.V.4.

accommodate those changes. The recently adopted UNCITRAL Expedited Arbitration Rules were particularly appropriate for low-value cases that were not overly complex, and might assist with the post-pandemic recovery by providing a mechanism to solve disputes more quickly, particularly those involving MSMEs, which were largely family-owned or owned by women, while also ensuring greater access to justice;

(g) In the area of secured transactions, legislative reforms based on UNCITRAL texts on secured transactions could have a positive impact on access to credit for MSMEs by facilitating the use of a wide range of movable assets as collateral.

313. The Commission also highlighted the launch of its first e-learning course, entitled "Introduction to the United Nations Commission on International Trade Law".[107] In addition to providing users with an introduction to legal harmonization and promoting international trade and the work of UNCITRAL, the course also outlined how UNCITRAL texts contributed to the achievement of the Sustainable Development Goals.

314. The Commission noted, as an example of the links between the Commission's work programme, the Sustainable Development Goals and the rule of law, the stocktaking project to compile, analyse and share relevant information regarding developments in dispute resolution in the digital economy. There had been a significant increase in the use of technology for resolving disputes through alternative dispute resolution, which had been accelerated by the pandemic. A wide range of technology was being employed to provide innovative dispute resolution services, thereby increasing access to services. Despite those benefits, the potential negative impacts of technology on the integrity of the process needed to be examined. Efforts should be made to ensure that the principle of due process and fairness are upheld. Another aspect deserving attention was the digital divide, that not all parties had access to the same technology. The use of technology also came at a cost, which might be burdensome for MSMEs, and it required a level of understanding that some individuals might not possess. Accordingly, the benefits that technology could bring needed to be weighed against such gaps to guarantee that technology could enhance access to justice for all. The outcome of the stocktaking project would not only assist the Commission in considering future work to be conducted in the area of dispute resolution but also provided the international community with concrete information on how technology could be utilized to improve dispute resolution and access to justice.

315. The Commission noted the expected contribution of its ongoing work on access to credit for MSMEs, early dismissal and preliminary determination in arbitration, investor-State dispute settlement reform, civil asset tracing and recovery in insolvency proceedings, and applicable law in insolvency proceedings to the achievement of the relevant Sustainable Development Goals.

XIX. Relevant General Assembly resolutions

316. The Commission recalled that, at its fiftieth session, in 2017, it had requested the secretariat to replace an oral report to the Commission on relevant General Assembly resolutions with a written report to be issued before the session.[108] Pursuant to that request, the Commission had before it at its fifty-fifth session a note by the Secretariat (A/CN.9/1104) summarizing the content of operative paragraphs of General Assembly resolutions 76/229 on the report of UNCITRAL on the work of its fifty-fourth session, 76/107 on the UNCITRAL Mediation Rules, 76/108 on the UNCITRAL Expedited Arbitration Rules and 76/109 on the enlargement of the membership of UNCITRAL.

317. The Commission took note of those General Assembly resolutions.

[107] The course can be accessed through the UNCITRAL website and on the e-campus website of the International Training Centre of the International Labour Organization. Access to and registration for the course is available at https://ecampus.itcilo.org/login/index.php.

[108] *Official Records of the General Assembly, Seventy-second Session, Supplement No. 17* (A/72/17), para. 480.

XX. Other business: evaluation of the role of the UNCITRAL secretariat in facilitating the work of the Commission

318. An online questionnaire on the level of satisfaction of UNCITRAL with the services provided by its secretariat was made available to States. The Commission was informed that 63 responses had been received and that the level of satisfaction with the services provided by the secretariat remained high. On average, respondents gave 4.73 out of 5 for "the services and support provided to the Commission", gave 4.76 out of 5 for "the availability of information on the UNCITRAL website" and gave 4.71 out of 5 for "the adaptability and responsiveness of the UNCITRAL secretariat to the challenges and circumstances arising from the COVID-19 pandemic".

319. The Commission expressed appreciation to its secretariat for its work.

XXI. Date and place of future meetings

A. Fifty-sixth session of the Commission

320. The Commission approved the holding of its fifty-sixth session in Vienna, from 3 to 21 July 2023.

B. Sessions of working groups

321. The Commission considered conference service requirements in the light of its work programme, reports of its working groups and a note by the Secretariat (A/CN.9/1103). It approved the following schedule of working group sessions in the second half of 2022 and 2023, noting that (a) the first day of the tentative dates of the seventy-eighth session of Working Group II (25 September 2023) would fall on Yom Kippur and (b) the last day of the tentative dates of the sixty-fifth session of Working Group IV (14 April 2023) would fall on Orthodox Good Friday, two of the significant holidays of the United Nations, unless alternative dates would be allocated to those working groups, taking into account their needs.

	Second half of 2022 (Vienna)	*First half of 2023 (New York)*	*Second half of 2023 (Vienna) (to be confirmed by the Commission at its fifty-sixth session, in 2023)*
Working Group I (MSMEs)	Thirty-eighth session 19–23 September 2022	Thirty-ninth session 13–17 February 2023	Fortieth session *18–22 September 2023*
Working Group II (Dispute Settlement)	Seventy-sixth session 10–14 October 2022	Seventy-seventh session 6–10 February 2023	Seventy-eighth session *25–29 September 2023 (falls on Yom Kippur)*
Working Group III (Investor-State Dispute Settlement Reform)	Forty-third session 5–16 September 2022	Forty-fourth session (Vienna) 23–27 January 2023 Forty-fifth session 27–31 March 2023	Forty-sixth session *9–13 October 2023*
Working Group IV (Electronic Commerce)	Sixty-fourth session 31 October–4 November 2022	Sixty-fifth session 10–14 April 2023 (falls on Orthodox Good Friday)	Sixty-sixth session *16–20 October 2023*
Working Group V (Insolvency Law)	Sixty-first session 12–16 December 2022	Sixty-second session 17–21 April 2023	Sixty-third session *11–15 December 2023*
Working Group VI (Negotiable multimodal transport documents)	Forty-first session 28 November–2 December 2022	Forty-second session 8–12 May 2023	Forty-third session *18–22 December 2023*

Annex I

Draft convention on the international effects of judicial sales of ships

The States Parties to this Convention,

Reaffirming their belief that international trade on the basis of equality and mutual benefit is an important element in promoting friendly relations among States,

Mindful of the crucial role of shipping in international trade and transportation, of the high economic value of ships used in both seagoing and inland navigation, and of the function of judicial sales as a means to enforce claims,

Considering that adequate legal protection for purchasers may positively impact the price realized at judicial sales of ships, to the benefit of both shipowners and creditors, including lienholders and ship financiers,

Wishing, for that purpose, to establish uniform rules that promote the dissemination of information on prospective judicial sales to interested parties and give international effects to judicial sales of ships sold free and clear of any mortgage or *hypothèque* and of any charge, including for ship registration purposes,

Have agreed as follows:

Article 1. Purpose

This Convention governs the international effects of a judicial sale of a ship that confers clean title on the purchaser.

Article 2. Definitions

For the purposes of this Convention:

(a) "Judicial sale" of a ship means any sale of a ship:

(i) Which is ordered, approved or confirmed by a court or other public authority either by way of public auction or by private treaty carried out under the supervision and with the approval of a court; and

(ii) For which the proceeds of sale are made available to the creditors;

(b) "Ship" means any ship or other vessel registered in a register that is open to public inspection that may be the subject of an arrest or other similar measure capable of leading to a judicial sale under the law of the State of judicial sale;

(c) "Clean title" means title free and clear of any mortgage or *hypothèque* and of any charge;

(d) "Mortgage or *hypothèque*" means any mortgage or *hypothèque* that is effected on a ship and registered in the State in whose register of ships or equivalent register the ship is registered;

(e) "Charge" means any right whatsoever and howsoever arising which may be asserted against a ship, whether by means of arrest, attachment or otherwise, and includes a maritime lien, lien, encumbrance, right of use or right of retention but does not include a mortgage or *hypothèque*;

(f) "Registered charge" means any charge that is registered in the register of ships or equivalent register in which the ship is registered or in any different register in which mortgages or *hypothèques* are registered;

(g) "Maritime lien" means any charge that is recognized as a maritime lien or *privilège maritime* on a ship under applicable law;

(h) "Owner" of a ship means any person registered as the owner of the ship in the register of ships or equivalent register in which the ship is registered;

(i) "Purchaser" means any person to whom the ship is sold in the judicial sale;

(j) "Subsequent purchaser" means the person who purchases the ship from the purchaser named in the certificate of judicial sale referred to in article 5;

(k) "State of judicial sale" means the State in which the judicial sale of a ship is conducted.

Article 3. Scope of application

1. This Convention applies only to a judicial sale of a ship if:

(a) The judicial sale is conducted in a State Party; and

(b) The ship is physically within the territory of the State of judicial sale at the time of that sale.

2. This Convention shall not apply to warships or naval auxiliaries, or other vessels owned or operated by a State and used, immediately prior to the time of judicial sale, only on government non-commercial service.

Article 4. Notice of judicial sale

1. The judicial sale shall be conducted in accordance with the law of the State of judicial sale, which shall also provide procedures for challenging the judicial sale prior to its completion and determine the time of the sale for the purposes of this Convention.

2. Notwithstanding paragraph 1, a certificate of judicial sale under article 5 shall only be issued if a notice of judicial sale is given prior to the judicial sale of the ship in accordance with the requirements of paragraphs 3 to 7.

3. The notice of judicial sale shall be given to:

(a) The registry of ships or equivalent registry with which the ship is registered;

(b) All holders of any mortgage or *hypothèque* and of any registered charge, provided that the register in which it is registered, and any instrument required to be registered under the law of the State of registration, are open to public inspection, and that extracts from the register and copies of such instruments are obtainable from the registry;

(c) All holders of any maritime lien, provided that they have notified the court or other public authority conducting the judicial sale of the claim secured by the maritime lien in accordance with the regulations and procedures of the State of judicial sale;

(d) The owner of the ship for the time being; and

(e) If the ship is granted bareboat charter registration:

(i) The person registered as the bareboat charterer of the ship in the bareboat charter register; and

(ii) The bareboat charter registry.

4. The notice of judicial sale shall be given in accordance with the law of the State of judicial sale, and shall contain, as a minimum, the information mentioned in annex I.

5. The notice of judicial sale shall also be:

(a) Published by announcement in the press or other publication available in the State of judicial sale; and

(b) Transmitted to the repository referred to in article 11 for publication.

6. For the purpose of communicating the notice to the repository, if the notice of judicial sale is not in a working language of the repository, it shall be accompanied by a translation of the information mentioned in annex I into any such working language.

7. In determining the identity or address of any person to whom the notice of judicial sale is to be given, it is sufficient to rely on:

(a) Information set forth in the register of ships or equivalent register in which the ship is registered or in the bareboat charter register;

(b) Information set forth in the register in which the mortgage or *hypothèque* or the registered charge is registered, if different to the register of ships or equivalent register; and

(c) Information notified under paragraph 3, subparagraph (c).

Article 5. Certificate of judicial sale

1. Upon completion of a judicial sale that conferred clean title to the ship under the law of the State of judicial sale and was conducted in accordance with the requirements of that law and the requirements of this Convention, the court or other public authority that conducted the judicial sale or other competent authority of the State of judicial sale shall, in accordance with its regulations and procedures, issue a certificate of judicial sale to the purchaser.

2. The certificate of judicial sale shall be substantially in the form of the model contained in annex II and contain:

(a) A statement that the ship was sold in accordance with the requirements of the law of the State of judicial sale and the requirements of this Convention;

(b) A statement that the judicial sale has conferred clean title to the ship on the purchaser;

(c) The name of the State of judicial sale;

(d) The name, address and the contact details of the authority issuing the certificate;

(e) The name of the court or other public authority that conducted the judicial sale and the date of the sale;

(f) The name of the ship and registry of ships or equivalent registry with which the ship is registered;

(g) The IMO number of the ship or, if not available, other information capable of identifying the ship;

(h) The name, address or residence or principal place of business of the owner of the ship immediately prior to the judicial sale;

(i) The name, address or residence or principal place of business of the purchaser;

(j) The place and date of issuance of the certificate; and

(k) The signature or stamp of the authority issuing the certificate or other confirmation of authenticity of the certificate.

3. The State of judicial sale shall require the certificate of judicial sale to be transmitted promptly to the repository referred to in article 11 for publication.

4. The certificate of judicial sale and any translation thereof shall be exempt from legalization or similar formality.

5. Without prejudice to articles 9 and 10, the certificate of judicial sale shall be sufficient evidence of the matters contained therein.

6. The certificate of judicial sale may be in the form of an electronic record provided that:

(a) The information contained therein is accessible so as to be usable for subsequent reference;

(b) A reliable method is used to identify the authority issuing the certificate; and

(c) A reliable method is used to detect any alteration to the record after the time it was generated, apart from the addition of any endorsement and any change that arises in the normal course of communication, storage and display.

7. A certificate of judicial sale shall not be rejected on the sole ground that it is in electronic form.

Article 6. International effects of a judicial sale

A judicial sale for which a certificate of judicial sale referred to in article 5 has been issued shall have the effect in every other State Party of conferring clean title to the ship on the purchaser.

Article 7. Action by the registry

1. At the request of the purchaser or subsequent purchaser and upon production of the certificate of judicial sale referred to in article 5, the registry or other competent authority of a State Party shall, as the case may be and in accordance with its regulations and procedures, but without prejudice to article 6:

(a) Delete from the register any mortgage or *hypothèque* and any registered charge attached to the ship that had been registered before completion of the judicial sale;

(b) Delete the ship from the register and issue a certificate of deletion for the purpose of new registration;

(c) Register the ship in the name of the purchaser or subsequent purchaser, provided further that the ship and the person in whose name the ship is to be registered meet the requirements of the law of the State of registration;

(d) Update the register with any other relevant particulars in the certificate of judicial sale.

2. At the request of the purchaser or subsequent purchaser and upon production of the certificate of judicial sale referred to in article 5, the registry or other competent authority of a State Party in which the ship was granted bareboat charter registration shall delete the ship from the bareboat charter register and issue a certificate of deletion.

3. If the certificate of judicial sale is not issued in an official language of the registry or other competent authority, the registry or other competent authority may request the purchaser or subsequent purchaser to produce a certified translation into such an official language.

4. The registry or other competent authority may also request the purchaser or subsequent purchaser to produce a certified copy of the certificate of judicial sale for its records.

5. Paragraphs 1 and 2 do not apply if a court in the State of the registry or of the other competent authority determines under article 10 that the effect of the judicial sale under article 6 would be manifestly contrary to the public policy of that State.

Article 8. No arrest of the ship

1. If an application is brought before a court or other judicial authority in a State Party to arrest a ship or to take any other similar measure against a ship for a claim

arising prior to a judicial sale of the ship, the court or other judicial authority shall, upon production of the certificate of judicial sale referred to in article 5, dismiss the application.

2. If a ship is arrested or a similar measure is taken against a ship by order of a court or other judicial authority in a State Party for a claim arising prior to a judicial sale of the ship, the court or other judicial authority shall, upon production of the certificate of judicial sale referred to in article 5, order the release of the ship.

3. If the certificate of judicial sale is not issued in an official language of the court or other judicial authority, the court or other judicial authority may request the person producing the certificate to produce a certified translation into such an official language.

4. Paragraphs 1 and 2 do not apply if the court or other judicial authority determines that dismissing the application or ordering the release of the ship, as the case may be, would be manifestly contrary to the public policy of that State.

Article 9. Jurisdiction to avoid and suspend judicial sale

1. The courts of the State of judicial sale shall have exclusive jurisdiction to hear any claim or application to avoid a judicial sale of a ship conducted in that State that confers clean title to the ship or to suspend its effects, which shall extend to any claim or application to challenge the issuance of the certificate of judicial sale referred to in article 5.

2. The courts of a State Party shall decline jurisdiction in respect of any claim or application to avoid a judicial sale of a ship conducted in another State Party that confers clean title to the ship or to suspend its effects.

3. The State of judicial sale shall require the decision of a court that avoids or suspends the effects of a judicial sale for which a certificate has been issued in accordance with article 5, paragraph 1, to be transmitted promptly to the repository referred to in article 11 for publication.

Article 10. Circumstances in which judicial sale has no international effect

A judicial sale of a ship shall not have the effect provided in article 6 in a State Party other than the State of judicial sale if a court in the other State Party determines that the effect would be manifestly contrary to the public policy of that other State Party.

Article 11. Repository

1. The repository shall be the Secretary-General of the International Maritime Organization or an institution named by the United Nations Commission on International Trade Law.

2. Upon receipt of a notice of judicial sale transmitted under article 4, paragraph 5, certificate of judicial sale transmitted under article 5, paragraph 3, or decision transmitted under article 9, paragraph 3, the repository shall make it available to the public in a timely manner, in the form and in the language in which it is received.

3. The repository may also receive a notice of judicial sale emanating from a State that has ratified, accepted, approved or acceded to this Convention and for which the Convention has not yet entered into force and may make it available to the public.

Article 12. Communication between authorities of States Parties

1. For the purposes of this Convention, the authorities of a State Party shall be authorized to correspond directly with the authorities of any other State Party.

2. Nothing in this article shall affect the application of any international agreement on judicial assistance in respect of civil and commercial matters that may exist between States Parties.

Article 13. Relationship with other international conventions

1. Nothing in this Convention shall affect the application of the Convention on the Registration of Inland Navigation Vessels (1965) and its Protocol No. 2 concerning Attachment and Forced Sale of Inland Navigation Vessels, including any future amendment to that convention or protocol.

2. Without prejudice to article 4, paragraph 4, as between States Parties to this Convention that are also parties to the Convention on the Service Abroad of Judicial and Extrajudicial Documents in Civil or Commercial Matters (1965), the notice of judicial sale may be transmitted abroad using channels other than those provided for in that convention.

Article 14. Other bases for giving international effect

Nothing in this Convention shall preclude a State from giving effect to a judicial sale of a ship conducted in another State under any other international agreement or under applicable law.

Article 15. Matters not governed by this Convention

1. Nothing in this Convention shall affect:

(a) The procedure for or priority in the distribution of proceeds of a judicial sale; or

(b) Any personal claim against a person who owned or had proprietary rights in the ship prior to the judicial sale.

2. Moreover, this Convention shall not govern the effects, under applicable law, of a decision by a court exercising jurisdiction under article 9, paragraph 1.

Article 16. Depositary

The Secretary-General of the United Nations is hereby designated as the depositary of this Convention.

Article 17. Signature, ratification, acceptance, approval, accession

1. This Convention is open for signature by all States in [Beijing], on [...], and thereafter at United Nations Headquarters in New York.

2. This Convention is subject to ratification, acceptance or approval by the signatory States.

3. This Convention is open for accession by all States that are not signatories as from the date it is open for signature.

4. Instruments of ratification, acceptance, approval or accession are to be deposited with the depositary.

Article 18. Participation by regional economic integration organizations

1. A regional economic integration organization that is constituted by sovereign States and has competence over certain matters governed by this Convention may similarly sign, ratify, accept, approve or accede to this Convention. The regional economic integration organization shall in that case have the rights and obligations of a State Party, to the extent that that organization has competence over matters governed by this Convention. For the purposes of articles 21 and 22, an instrument deposited by a regional economic integration organization shall not be counted in addition to the instruments deposited by its member States.

2. The regional economic integration organization shall make a declaration specifying the matters governed by this Convention in respect of which competence has been transferred to that organization by its member States. The regional economic integration organization shall promptly notify the depositary of any changes to the

distribution of competence, including new transfers of competence, specified in the declaration under this paragraph.

3. Any reference to a "State", "States", "State Party" or "States Parties" in this Convention applies equally to a regional economic integration organization where the context so requires.

4. This Convention shall not affect the application of rules of a regional economic integration organization, whether adopted before or after this Convention:

(a) In relation to the transmission of a notice of judicial sale between member States of such an organization; or

(b) In relation to the jurisdictional rules applicable between member States of such an organization.

Article 19. Non-unified legal systems

1. If a State has two or more territorial units in which different systems of law are applicable in relation to the matters dealt with in this Convention, it may declare that this Convention shall extend to all its territorial units or only to one or more of them.

2. Declarations under this article shall state expressly the territorial units to which this Convention extends.

3. If a State makes no declaration under paragraph 1, this Convention shall extend to all territorial units of that State.

4. If a State has two or more territorial units in which different systems of law are applicable in relation to the matters dealt with in this Convention:

(a) Any reference to the law, regulations or procedures of the State shall be construed as referring, where appropriate, to the law, regulations or procedures in force in the relevant territorial unit;

(b) Any reference to the authority of the State shall be construed as referring, where appropriate, to the authority in the relevant territorial unit.

Article 20. Procedure and effects of declarations

1. Declarations under article 18, paragraph 2, and article 19, paragraph 1, shall be made at the time of signature, ratification, acceptance, approval or accession. Declarations made at the time of signature are subject to confirmation upon ratification, acceptance or approval.

2. Declarations and their confirmations shall be in writing and formally notified to the depositary.

3. A declaration takes effect simultaneously with the entry into force of this Convention in respect of the State concerned.

4. Any State that makes a declaration under article 18, paragraph 2, and article 19, paragraph 1, may modify or withdraw it at any time by a formal notification in writing addressed to the depositary. The modification or withdrawal shall take effect 180 days after the date of the receipt of the notification by the depositary. If the depositary receives the notification of the modification or withdrawal before entry into force of this Convention in respect of the State concerned, the modification or withdrawal shall take effect simultaneously with the entry into force of this Convention in respect of that State.

Article 21. Entry into force

1. This Convention shall enter into force 180 days after the date of the deposit of the third instrument of ratification, acceptance, approval or accession.

2. When a State ratifies, accepts, approves or accedes to this Convention after the deposit of the third instrument of ratification, acceptance, approval or accession, this

Convention shall enter into force in respect of that State 180 days after the date of the deposit of its instrument of ratification, acceptance, approval or accession.

3. This Convention shall apply only to judicial sales ordered or approved after its entry into force in respect of the State of judicial sale.

Article 22. Amendment

1. Any State Party may propose an amendment to this Convention by submitting it to the Secretary-General of the United Nations. The Secretary-General shall thereupon communicate the proposed amendment to the States Parties with a request that they indicate whether they favour a conference of States Parties for the purpose of considering and voting upon the proposal. In the event that within 120 days from the date of such communication at least one third of the States Parties favour such a conference, the Secretary-General shall convene the conference under the auspices of the United Nations.

2. The conference of States Parties shall make every effort to achieve consensus on each amendment. If all efforts at consensus are exhausted and no consensus is reached, the amendment shall, as a last resort, require for its adoption a two-thirds majority vote of the States Parties present and voting at the conference. For the purposes of this paragraph, the vote of a regional economic integration organization shall not be counted.

3. An adopted amendment shall be submitted by the depositary to all States Parties for ratification, acceptance or approval.

4. An adopted amendment shall enter into force 180 days after the date of deposit of the third instrument of ratification, acceptance or approval. When an amendment enters into force, it shall be binding on those States Parties that have expressed consent to be bound by it.

5. When a State Party ratifies, accepts or approves an amendment following the deposit of the third instrument of ratification, acceptance or approval, the amendment shall enter into force in respect of that State Party 180 days after the date of the deposit of its instrument of ratification, acceptance or approval.

Article 23. Denunciation

1. A State Party may denounce this Convention by a formal notification in writing addressed to the depositary. The denunciation may be limited to certain territorial units of a non-unified legal system to which this Convention applies.

2. The denunciation shall take effect 365 days after the date of the receipt of the notification by the depositary. Where a longer period for the denunciation to take effect is specified in the notification, the denunciation shall take effect upon the expiration of such longer period after the date of the receipt of the notification by the depositary. This Convention shall continue to apply to a judicial sale for which a certificate of judicial sale referred to in article 5 has been issued before the denunciation takes effect.

DONE at [Beijing] this [...] day of [...], in a single original, of which the Arabic, Chinese, English, French, Russian and Spanish texts are equally authentic.

Annex I

Minimum information to be contained in the notice of judicial sale

1. Statement that the notice of judicial sale is given for the purposes of the United Nations Convention on the International Effects of Judicial Sales of Ships

2. Name of State of judicial sale

3. Court or other public authority ordering, approving or confirming the judicial sale

4. Reference number or other identifier for the judicial sale procedure

5. Name of ship

6. Registry

7. IMO number

8. (*If IMO number not available*) Other information capable of identifying the ship

9. Name of the owner

10. Address or residence or principal place of business of the owner

11. (*If judicial sale by public auction*) Anticipated date, time and place of public auction

12. (*If judicial sale by private treaty*) Any relevant details, including time period, for the judicial sale as ordered by the court or other public authority

13. Statement either confirming that the judicial sale will confer clean title to the ship, or, if it is not known whether the judicial sale will confer clean title, a statement of the circumstances under which the judicial sale would not confer clean title

14. Other information required by the law of the State of judicial sale, in particular any information deemed necessary to protect the interests of the person receiving the notice

Annex II

Model certificate of judicial sale

Issued in accordance with the provisions of article 5 of the United Nations Convention on the International Effects of Judicial Sales of Ships

This is to certify that:

(a) The ship described below was sold by way of judicial sale in accordance with the requirements of the law of the State of judicial sale and the requirements of the United Nations Convention on the International Effects of Judicial Sales of Ships; and

(b) The judicial sale has conferred clean title to the ship on the purchaser.

1.	**State of judicial sale**	....
2.	**Authority issuing this certificate**	
2.1	Name	....
2.2	Address	....
2.3	Telephone/fax/email, if available	....
3.	**Judicial sale**	
3.1	Name of court or other public authority that conducted the judicial sale	....
3.2	Date of the judicial sale	....
4.	**Ship**	
4.1	Name	....
4.2	Registry	....
4.3	IMO number	....
4.4	(*If IMO number not available*) Other information capable of identifying the ship	(*Please attach any photos to the certificate*) ....
5.	**Owner immediately prior to the judicial sale**	
5.1	Name	....
5.2	Address or residence or principal place of business	....
6.	**Purchaser**	
6.1	Name	....
6.2	Address or residence or principal place of business	....

At... (place)

On .... (date)

....

Signature and/or stamp of issuing authority or other confirmation of authenticity of the certificate

Annex II

UNCITRAL Model Law on the Use and Cross-border Recognition of Identity Management and Trust Services

Chapter I. General provisions

Article 1. Definitions

For the purposes of this Law:

(a) "Attribute" means an item of information or data associated with a person;

(b) "Data message" means information generated, sent, received or stored by electronic, magnetic, optical or similar means;

(c) "Electronic identification", in the context of identity management services, means a process used to achieve sufficient assurance in the binding between a person and an identity;

(d) "Identity" means a set of attributes that allows a person to be uniquely distinguished within a particular context;

(e) "Identity credentials" means the data, or the physical object upon which the data may reside, that a person may present for electronic identification;

(f) "Identity management services" means services consisting of managing identity proofing and electronic identification;

(g) "Identity management service provider" means a person who enters into an arrangement for the provision of identity management services with a subscriber;

(h) "Identity management system" means a set of functions and capabilities to manage identity proofing and electronic identification;

(i) "Identity proofing" means the process of collecting, verifying, and validating sufficient attributes to define and confirm the identity of a person within a particular context;

(j) "Relying party" means a person who acts on the basis of the result of identity management services or trust services;

(k) "Subscriber" means a person who enters into an arrangement for the provision of identity management services or trust services with an identity management service provider or a trust service provider;

(l) "Trust service" means an electronic service that provides assurance of certain qualities of a data message and includes the methods for creating and managing electronic signatures, electronic seals, electronic time stamps, website authentication, electronic archiving and electronic registered delivery services;

(m) "Trust service provider" means a person who enters into an arrangement for the provision of one or more trust services with a subscriber.

Article 2. Scope of application

1. This Law applies to the use and cross-border recognition of identity management and trust services in the context of commercial activities and trade-related services.

2. Nothing in this Law requires the identification of a person.

3. Nothing in this Law affects a legal requirement that a person be identified or that a trust service be used in accordance with a procedure defined or prescribed by law.

4. Other than as provided for in this Law, nothing in this Law affects the application to identity management services or trust services of any law applicable to data privacy and protection.

Article 3. Voluntary use of identity management and trust services

1. Nothing in this Law requires a person to use an identity management service or trust service or to use a particular identity management service or trust service without the person's consent.

2. For the purposes of paragraph 1, consent may be inferred from the person's conduct.

Article 4. Interpretation

1. In the interpretation of this Law, regard is to be had to its international origin and to the need to promote uniformity in its application and the observance of good faith in international trade.

2. Questions concerning matters governed by this Law which are not expressly settled in it are to be settled in conformity with the general principles on which it is based.

Chapter II. Identity management

Article 5. Legal recognition of identity management

Subject to article 2, paragraph 3, the result of electronic identification shall not be denied legal effect, validity, enforceability or admissibility as evidence on the sole ground that:

(a) The identity proofing and electronic identification are in electronic form; or

(b) The identity management system is not designated pursuant to article 11.

Article 6. Obligations of identity management service providers

An identity management service provider shall, at a minimum:

(a) Have in place operational rules, policies and practices, as appropriate to the purpose and design of the identity management system, to address, at a minimum, requirements to:

(i) Enrol persons, including by:

a. Registering and collecting attributes;

b. Carrying out identity proofing and verification; and

c. Binding the identity credentials to the person;

(ii) Update attributes;

(iii) Manage identity credentials, including by:

a. Issuing, delivering and activating credentials;

b. Suspending, revoking and reactivating credentials; and

c. Renewing and replacing credentials;

(iv) Manage the electronic identification of persons, including by:

a. Managing electronic identification factors; and

b. Managing electronic identification mechanisms;

(b) Act in accordance with its operational rules, policies and practices, and any representations that it makes with respect to them;

(c) Ensure the online availability and correct operation of the identity management system;

(d) Make its operational rules, policies and practices easily accessible to subscribers, relying parties and other third parties;

(e) Provide easily accessible means that enable a relying party to ascertain, where relevant:

(i) Any limitation on the purpose or value for which the identity management service may be used; and

(ii) Any limitation on the scope or extent of liability stipulated by the identity management service provider; and

(f) Provide and make publicly available means by which a subscriber may notify the identity management service provider of a security breach pursuant to article 8.

Article 7. Obligations of identity management service providers in case of data breach

1. If a breach of security or loss of integrity occurs that has a significant impact on the identity management system, including the attributes managed therein, the identity management service provider shall, in accordance with the law:

(a) Take all reasonable steps to contain the breach or loss, including, where appropriate, suspending the affected service or revoking the affected identity credentials;

(b) Remedy the breach or loss; and

(c) Notify the breach or loss.

2. If a person notifies the identity management service provider of a breach of security or loss of integrity, the identity management service provider shall:

(a) Investigate the potential breach or loss; and

(b) Take any other appropriate action under paragraph 1.

Article 8. Obligations of subscribers

The subscriber shall notify the identity management service provider, by utilizing means made available by the identity management service provider pursuant to article 6 or by otherwise using reasonable means, if:

(a) The subscriber knows that the subscriber's identity credentials have been compromised; or

(b) The circumstances known to the subscriber give rise to a substantial risk that the subscriber's identity credentials may have been compromised.

Article 9. Identification of a person using identity management

Subject to article 2, paragraph 3, where the law requires the identification of a person for a particular purpose, or provides consequences for the absence of identification, that requirement is met with respect to identity management services if a reliable method in accordance with article 10, paragraph 1, or article 10, paragraph 4, is used for the identity proofing and electronic identification of the person for that purpose.

Article 10. Reliability requirements for identity management services

1. For the purposes of article 9, the method shall be:

(a) As reliable as appropriate for the purpose for which the identity management service is being used; or

(b) Deemed to be as reliable as appropriate if proven in fact by or before a court or competent adjudicative body to have fulfilled the function described in article 9, by itself or together with further evidence.

2. In determining the reliability of the method, all relevant circumstances shall be taken into account, which may include:

(a) Compliance of the identity management service provider with the obligations listed in article 6;

(b) Compliance of the operational rules, policies and practices of the identity management service provider with any applicable recognized international standards and procedures relevant for the provision of identity management services, including level of assurance frameworks, in particular rules on:

(i) Governance;

(ii) Published notices and user information;

(iii) Information security management;

(iv) Record-keeping;

(v) Facilities and staff;

(vi) Technical controls; and

(vii) Oversight and audit;

(c) Any supervision or certification provided with regard to the identity management service;

(d) Any relevant level of assurance of the method used;

(e) The purpose for which identification is being used; and

(f) Any relevant agreement between the parties, including any limitation on the purpose or value of the transactions for which the identity management service might be used.

3. In determining the reliability of the method, no regard shall be had:

(a) To the geographic location where the identity management service is provided; or

(b) To the geographic location of the place of business of the identity management service provider.

4. A method used by an identity management service designated pursuant to article 11 is presumed to be reliable.

5. Paragraph 4 does not limit the ability of any person:

(a) To establish in any other way the reliability of a method; or

(b) To adduce evidence of the non-reliability of a method used by an identity management service designated pursuant to article 11.

Article 11. Designation of reliable identity management services

1. [*A person, organ or authority, whether public or private, specified by the enacting jurisdiction as competent*] may designate identity management services that are presumed reliable.

2. The [*person, organ or authority, whether public or private, specified by the enacting jurisdiction as competent*] shall:

(a) Take into account all relevant circumstances, including the factors listed in article 10, in designating an identity management service; and

(b) Publish a list of designated identity management services, including details of the identity management service provider.

3. Any designation pursuant to paragraph 1 shall be consistent with recognized international standards and procedures relevant for performing the designation process, including level of assurance frameworks.

4. In designating an identity management service, no regard shall be had:

(a) To the geographic location where the identity management service is provided; or

(b) To the geographic location of the place of business of the identity management service provider.

Article 12. Liability of identity management service providers

1. The identity management service provider shall be liable for loss caused to the subscriber or to the relying party due to a failure to comply with its obligations under articles 6 and 7.

2. Paragraph 1 shall be applied in accordance with rules on liability under the law and is without prejudice to:

(a) Any other basis of liability under the law, including liability for failure to comply with contractual obligations; or

(b) Any other legal consequences of a failure of the identity management service provider to comply with its obligations under this Law.

3. Notwithstanding paragraph 1, the identity management service provider shall not be liable to a subscriber for loss arising from the use of an identity management service to the extent that:

(a) That use exceeds the limitations on the purpose or value of the transaction for which the identity management service is used; and

(b) Those limitations are contained in the arrangement between the identity management service provider and the subscriber.

4. Notwithstanding paragraph 1, the identity management service provider shall not be liable to a relying party for loss arising from the use of an identity management service to the extent that:

(a) That use exceeds the limitations on the purpose or value of the transaction for which the identity management service is used; and

(b) The identity management service provider has complied with its obligations under article 6, subparagraph (e), with respect to that transaction.

Chapter III. Trust services

Article 13. Legal recognition of trust services

The result deriving from the use of a trust service shall not be denied legal effect, validity, enforceability or admissibility as evidence on the sole ground that:

(a) It is in electronic form; or

(b) The trust service is not designated pursuant to article 23.

Article 14. Obligations of trust service providers

1. A trust service provider shall, at a minimum:

(a) Have in place operational rules, policies and practices, including a plan to ensure continuity in case of termination of activity, as appropriate to the purpose and design of the trust service;

(b) Act in accordance with its operational rules, policies and practices, and any representations that it makes with respect to them;

(c) Make its operational rules, policies and practices easily accessible to subscribers, relying parties and other third parties;

(d) Provide and make publicly available means by which a subscriber may notify the trust service provider of a security breach pursuant to article 15; and

(e) Provide easily accessible means that enable a relying party to ascertain, where relevant:

(i) Any limitation on the purpose or value for which the trust service may be used; and

(ii) Any limitation on the scope or extent of liability stipulated by the trust service provider.

2. If a breach of security or loss of integrity occurs that has a significant impact on a trust service, the trust service provider shall, in accordance with the law:

(a) Take all reasonable steps to contain the breach or loss, including, where appropriate, suspending or revoking the affected service;

(b) Remedy the breach or loss; and

(c) Notify the breach or loss.

Article 15. Obligations of subscribers

The subscriber shall notify the trust service provider, by utilizing means made available by the trust service provider pursuant to article 14, paragraph 1, or by otherwise using reasonable means, if:

(a) The subscriber knows that data or means used by the subscriber for access and usage of the trust service have been compromised; or

(b) The circumstances known to the subscriber give rise to a substantial risk that the trust service may have been compromised.

Article 16. Electronic signatures

Where the law requires a signature of a person, or provides consequences for the absence of a signature, that requirement is met in relation to a data message if a reliable method in accordance with article 22, paragraph 1, or article 22, paragraph 4, is used:

(a) To identify the person; and

(b) To indicate the person's intention in respect of the information contained in the data message.

Article 17. Electronic seals

Where the law requires a legal person to affix a seal, or provides consequences for the absence of a seal, that requirement is met in relation to a data message if a reliable method in accordance with article 22, paragraph 1, or article 22, paragraph 4, is used:

(a) To provide reliable assurance of the origin of the data message; and

(b) To detect any alteration to the data message after the time and date of affixation, apart from the addition of any endorsement and any change that arises in the normal course of communication, storage and display.

Article 18. Electronic timestamps

Where the law requires a document, record, information or data to be associated with a time and date, or provides consequences for the absence of a time and date, that requirement is met in relation to a data message if a reliable method in accordance with article 22, paragraph 1, or article 22, paragraph 4, is used:

(a) To indicate the time and date, including by reference to the time zone; and

(b) To associate that time and date with the data message.

Article 19. Electronic archiving

Where the law requires a document, record or information to be retained, or provides consequences for the absence of retention, that requirement is met in relation to a data message if a reliable method in accordance with article 22, paragraph 1, or article 22, paragraph 4, is used:

(a) To make the information contained in the data message accessible so as to be usable for subsequent reference;

(b) To indicate the time and date of archiving and associate that time and date with the data message;

(c) To retain the data message in the format in which it was generated, sent or received, or in another format which can be demonstrated to detect any alteration to the data message after that time and date, apart from the addition of any endorsement and any change that arises in the normal course of communication, storage and display; and

(d) To retain such information, if any, as enables the identification of the origin and destination of a data message and the time and date when it was sent or received.

Article 20. Electronic registered delivery services

Where the law requires a document, record or information to be delivered by registered mail or similar service, or provides consequences for the absence of delivery, that requirement is met in relation to a data message if a reliable method in accordance with article 22, paragraph 1, or article 22, paragraph 4, is used:

(a) To indicate the time and date when the data message was received for delivery and the time and date when it was delivered;

(b) To detect any alteration to the data message after the time and date when the data message was received for delivery to the time and date when it was delivered, apart from the addition of any endorsement or information required by this article, and any change that arises in the normal course of communication, storage and display; and

(c) To identify the sender and the recipient.

Article 21. Website authentication

Where the law requires website authentication, or provides consequences for the absence of website authentication, that requirement is met if a reliable method in accordance with article 22, paragraph 1, or article 22, paragraph 4, is used:

(a) To identify the person who holds the domain name for the website; and

(b) To associate that person with the website.

Article 22. Reliability requirements for trust services

1. For the purposes of articles 16 to 21, the method shall be:

(a) As reliable as appropriate for the purpose for which the trust service is being used; or

(b) Deemed to be as reliable as appropriate if proven in fact by or before a court or competent adjudicative body to have fulfilled the functions described in the article, by itself or together with further evidence.

2. In determining the reliability of the method, all relevant circumstances shall be taken into account, which may include:

(a) Compliance of the trust service provider with the obligations listed in article 14;

(b) Compliance of the operational rules, policies and practices of the trust service provider with any applicable recognized international standards and procedures relevant for the provision of trust services;

(c) Any relevant level of reliability of the method used;

(d) Any applicable industry standard;

(e) The security of hardware and software;

(f) Financial and human resources, including the existence of assets;

(g) The regularity and extent of audit by an independent body;

(h) The existence of a declaration by a supervisory body, an accreditation body or a voluntary scheme regarding the reliability of the method;

(i) The purpose for which the trust service is being used; and

(j) Any relevant agreement between the parties, including any limitation on the purpose or value of the transactions for which the trust service might be used.

3. In determining the reliability of the method, no regard shall be had:

(a) To the geographic location where the trust service is provided; or

(b) To the geographic location of the place of business of the trust service provider.

4. A method used by a trust service designated pursuant to article 23 is presumed to be reliable.

5. Paragraph 4 does not limit the ability of any person:

(a) To establish in any other way the reliability of a method; or

(b) To adduce evidence of the non-reliability of a method used by a trust service designated pursuant to article 23.

Article 23. Designation of reliable trust services

1. [A person, organ or authority, whether public or private, specified by the enacting jurisdiction as competent] may designate trust services that are presumed reliable.

2. The [*person, organ or authority, whether public or private, specified by the enacting jurisdiction as competent*] shall:

(a) Take into account all relevant circumstances, including the factors listed in article 22, in designating a trust service; and

(b) Publish a list of designated trust services, including details of the trust service provider.

3. Any designation pursuant to paragraph 1 shall be consistent with recognized international standards and procedures relevant for performing the designation process.

4. In designating a trust service, no regard shall be had:

(a) To the geographic location where the trust service is provided; or

(b) To the geographic location of the place of business of the trust service provider.

Article 24. Liability of trust service providers

1. The trust service provider shall be liable for loss caused to the subscriber or to the relying party due to a failure to comply with its obligations under article 14.

2. Paragraph 1 shall be applied in accordance with rules on liability under the law and is without prejudice to:

(a) any other basis of liability under the law, including liability for failure to comply with contractual obligations; or

(b) any other legal consequences of a failure of the trust service provider to comply with its obligations under this Law.

3. Notwithstanding paragraph 1, the trust service provider shall not be liable to a subscriber for loss arising from the use of a trust service to the extent that:

(a) That use exceeds the limitations on the purpose or value of the transaction for which the trust service is used; and

(b) Those limitations are contained in the arrangement between the trust service provider and the subscriber.

4. Notwithstanding paragraph 1, the trust service provider shall not be liable to a relying party for loss arising from the use of a trust service to the extent that:

(a) That use exceeds the limitations on the purpose or value of the transaction for which the trust service is used; and

(b) The trust service provider has complied with its obligations under article 14, subparagraph 1(e) with respect to that transaction.

Chapter IV. Cross-border recognition

Article 25. Cross-border recognition of electronic identification

1. The result of electronic identification provided outside [*the enacting jurisdiction*] shall have the same legal effect in [*the enacting jurisdiction*] as electronic identification provided in [*the enacting jurisdiction*] if the method used by the identity management system, identity management service, or identity credential, as appropriate, offers:

(a) At least an equivalent level of assurance, where the assurance levels recognized by such jurisdictions are identical; or

(b) Substantially equivalent or higher level of assurance, in all other cases.

2. For the purposes of determining satisfaction of paragraph 1, regard shall be had to recognized international standards.

3. An identity management system, identity management service or identity credential shall be presumed to satisfy paragraph 1 if [*the person, organ or authority specified by the enacting jurisdiction pursuant to article 11*] has determined the equivalence, taking into account article 10, paragraph 2.

Article 26. Cross-border recognition of the result of the use of trust services

1. The result deriving from the use of a trust service provided outside [*the enacting jurisdiction*] shall have the same legal effect in [*the enacting jurisdiction*] as the result

deriving from the use of a trust service provided in [*the enacting jurisdiction*] if the method used by the trust service offers:

(a) At least an equivalent level of reliability, where the reliability levels recognized by such jurisdictions are identical; or

(b) Substantially equivalent or higher level of reliability, in all other cases.

2. For the purposes of determining satisfaction of paragraph 1, regard shall be had to recognized international standards.

3. The trust service shall be presumed to satisfy paragraph 1 if [*the person, organ or authority specified by the enacting jurisdiction pursuant to article 23*] has determined the equivalence, taking into account article 22, paragraph 2.

Article 27. Cooperation

[*The person, organ or authority specified by the enacting jurisdiction as competent*] may cooperate with foreign entities by exchanging information, experience and good practice relating to identity management and trust services, in particular with respect to:

(a) Recognition of the legal effects of foreign identity management systems and trust services, whether granted unilaterally or by mutual agreement;

(b) Designation of identity management systems and trust services; and

(c) Definition of levels of assurance of identity management systems and of levels of reliability of trust services.

Annex III

Recommendations to assist mediation centres and other interested bodies with regard to mediation under the UNCITRAL Mediation Rules (2021)

I. Introduction

A. The UNCITRAL Mediation Rules (2021)

1. The UNCITRAL Mediation Rules (2021) (the "Rules") provide a comprehensive set of procedural rules upon which parties may agree for the conduct of mediation proceedings arising out of their relationship. The Rules cover all aspects of the mediation process: they define when mediation is deemed to have commenced and terminated, address the appointment and role of mediators, and provide for the general conduct of mediation. A model mediation clause is also attached to the Rules.

2. The Rules are the result of a revision of the 1980 UNCITRAL Conciliation Rules, undertaken to ensure consistency with the provisions of the United Nations Convention on International Settlement Agreements Resulting from Mediation (the Singapore Convention on Mediation) and the Model Law on International Commercial Mediation and International Settlement Agreements Resulting from Mediation (2018) (the "2018 Model Law on Mediation"), both finalized by the Commission at its fifty-first session in 2018.[1] Revision of the 1980 Conciliation Rules was also considered appropriate in the light of developments in the field of mediation since 1980, including the development of court-ordered mediation.[2]

3. Until 2018, UNCITRAL primarily used the term "conciliation" with the understanding that the terms "conciliation" and "mediation" were interchangeable. In preparing the Singapore Convention on Mediation and the 2018 Model Law on Mediation, the Commission decided to use the term "mediation" to adapt the terminology to the current use and with the expectation that that terminology would simplify the promotion and heighten the visibility of the instruments developed by UNCITRAL in the area of mediation. The change in terminology is not meant to have any substantive or conceptual implications.[3]

B. Purpose of the recommendations

4. These recommendations are intended to inform and assist mediation centres and other interested bodies (hereinafter referred to generally as "institutions") that envisage using the Rules in the institutional context. In particular, the Rules could:

(a) Serve as a model for institutions drafting their own mediation rules, the degree to which can range from inspiration to full adoption of the Rules (see chapter II below);

(b) Be utilized by institutions in offering to administer disputes under the Rules (or when requested by the parties to do so) or rendering administrative and logistical services in ad hoc mediation under the Rules (see chapter III below); or

(c) Enable institutions to appoint a mediator or mediators upon request by the parties, as provided by, and in accordance with, the Rules (see chapter IV below).

---

[1] *Official Records of the General Assembly, Seventy-third Session, Supplement No. 17* (A/73/17), paras. 246 and 254.

[2] A/CN.9/1026, para. 5.

[3] *Official Records of the General Assembly, Seventy-third Session Supplement No. 17* (A/73/17), para. 19.

II. Adoption of the UNCITRAL Mediation Rules (2021) as the institutional rules of institutions

A. Substance of the UNCITRAL Mediation Rules (2021)

5. Institutions, when preparing or revising their institutional rules, may wish to consider using the Rules as a model. An institution that intends to do so should take into account the expectations of the parties that the rules of the institution will faithfully follow the text of the Rules (see paras. 7 and 8 below). In such cases, the institutional rules could provide as follows:

> "The present [*name of the institution's institutional rules*] are based on the UNCITRAL Mediation Rules (2021)."

6. This appeal to follow closely the substance of the Rules does not mean that the particular organizational structure, the unique circumstances of a country, region or jurisdiction, and the needs of a given institution could not be taken into account. Institutions adopting the Rules as their institutional rules will understandably need to comply with the national legal framework, and add, delete or further modify provisions, for instance, on administrative services or fee schedules (see paras. 13–16 below). In addition, potential modifications affecting some provisions of the Rules, as indicated below in paragraphs 9 to 19, may also be taken into account.

B. Presentation of possible adjustments

1. A short explanation

7. If an institution uses the Rules as a model for drafting its own institutional rules, it may be useful for the institution to consider referring to the Rules and indicating where their rules diverge from the Rules. Such indications may be helpful to potential users of those institutional rules who would otherwise have to embark on a comparative analysis to identify any disparity.

8. The institution may wish to include a text, for example, after the sentence outlined in paragraph 5, which refers to the specific provisions in the institutional rules that diverge from the Rules. Furthermore, it may be advisable to prepare a short explanation of the reasons for such modifications, which could accompany the institutional rules.

2. Right of parties to exclude or vary provisions of the UNCITRAL Mediation Rules at any time

9. The right of the parties to agree to exclude or vary provisions of the Rules at any time as prescribed by article 1, paragraph 4, may oblige institutions to administer mediations under provisions that are inconsistent with their institutional approach. Therefore, institutions may wish to consider amending article 1, paragraph 4, as follows:

> "The parties may agree in writing, in consultation with the mediator where one has been appointed, to exclude or vary any provision of the [*name of the institutional rules*] at any time. [*Name of institution*] may refuse to administer mediations under the [*name of the institutional rules*] if any agreed variations are incompatible with [*name of institution*]'s approach to consensual dispute resolution."

3. Communication

10. When an institution administers mediation, the initial communication between the parties is often carried out through the institution.[4] Therefore, it is recommended that institutions adapt article 2, paragraph 2, of the Rules relating to any invitations from one party to the other party to engage in mediation. Article 2, paragraph 2, may be amended as follows:

> "If the party that invited another party to mediate does not receive an acceptance of the invitation within 30 days from the day on which the invitation was sent by [*name of the institution*] through any means that provides for a record of its transmission, or within such other period of time as specified in the invitation, that party may elect to treat this as non-acceptance of the invitation to mediate. In such circumstances, [*name of institution*] may provide evidence of such an attempt to mediate upon request of any of the parties."

4. Reference to the institution for the appointment of a mediator

11. The institution may assist the parties by recommending and selecting a mediator under its institutional rules upon request by the parties. For this purpose, institutions should amend the following provisions of the Rules:

(a) Article 3, paragraph 3: "The parties may seek the assistance of [*name of institution*] for appointing a mediator.";

(b) The chapeau of article 3, paragraph 4: "In recommending or selecting individuals to act as mediator, [*name of institution*] shall have regard to ...";

(c) Article 3, paragraph 5: "If the parties have different nationalities, [*name of institution*] may also take into account the advisability of appointing a mediator of a nationality other than the nationalities of the parties in consultation with the parties. In addition, [*name of institution*], in selecting a mediator, shall take into consideration geographical diversity and gender of the candidates.".

12. Moreover, in the light of the role of the institution as the administrator of the mediation, it is recommended that article 4, paragraph 3 (b), be deleted.

5. Fees and schedule of fees

13. Where an institution wishes to adopt the Rules as its own institutional rules, and if the institution charges a fee for the administration, it may wish to amend article 11, paragraph 1 (d), as follows:

> "The cost of any assistance provided by [*name of institution*] including those pursuant to article 3, paragraph 3, and article 4, paragraph 3, of the [*name of the institutional rules*]."

14. If an institution wishes to administer all costs, it may wish to amend article 11, paragraph 1, as follows:

> "[*Name of the institution*] shall determine a preliminary advance on costs for the prospective administrative fees of [*name of the institution*], the down payment on the mediator's fees and the anticipated expenses (such as travel and subsistence costs of the mediator, delivery charges, rent, etc.) as early as possible in the mediation. Upon termination of the mediation, [*name of institution*] shall fix the costs of the mediation, which shall be reasonable in

[4] It is also possible for the institution to take charge of the correspondence throughout the proceedings between the parties and between the parties and the mediator as part of their services, which would consequently require further amendments, notably to articles 2, 3, paragraph 6, and 4, paragraph 5, as well as the need to add a rule governing the exchange of documents. Any variation or adaption should not affect article 5, which is a core element of the mediation.

amount and give written notice thereof to the parties. The term "costs" includes only:

(a) The fees of the mediator;

(b) The travel and other expenses of the mediator;

(c) The cost of expert advice requested by the mediator with the agreement of the parties;

(d) The cost of any assistance provided by [*name of institution*] including those pursuant to article 3, paragraph 3 and article 4, paragraph 3, of the [*name of the institutional rules*]; and

(e) Any other expenses that may have been accrued out of the mediation, including in relation to translation and interpretation services."

15. Article 11, paragraphs 3–6, might be amended as follows:

"[*Name of institution*], upon appointment, may request each party to deposit an equal amount in advance for the costs referred to in paragraph 1, unless otherwise agreed by the parties and the mediator."

"During the course of the mediation, [*name of institution*] may request supplementary deposits in an equal amount from each party, unless otherwise agreed by the parties and the mediator."

"If the required deposits under paragraphs 3 and 4 are not paid in full by all parties within a reasonable period set by [*name of institution*], [*name of institution*] may suspend the mediation or may declare the termination of the mediation, in accordance with article 9, subparagraph (e)."

"Upon termination of the mediation and if deposits were received, the [*name of institution*] shall render an accounting to the parties of the deposits received and return any unexpended funds to the parties."

16. Additionally, in case the institution chooses the option in paragraphs 13–15 above, the institution would need to adapt article 9, subparagraph (e), accordingly:

"By a declaration of [*name of institution*], after consultation with the parties, in the situation referred to in article 11, paragraph 5, on the date of the declaration;"

6. Form requirement of settlement agreements

17. In order to allow parties to provide evidence that a settlement agreement resulted from mediation, which may, for example, be required at the enforcement stage, and in accordance with article 4, paragraph 1 (b), of the Singapore Convention on Mediation, the institution may wish to provide an attestation and amend article 8, paragraph 2, accordingly:

"[*Name of institution*] shall upon the request of either party provide an attestation that the settlement agreement resulted from mediation."

7. Staff of the institution as witness

18. The institution might further add a prohibition to call representatives of the institution or its employees as witnesses in any further proceedings. Article 12, paragraph 3, may be amended as follows:

"The parties shall not present the mediator, representatives of [*name of institution*], or its employees or any participant in the mediation as witnesses in any such proceedings."

8. Exclusion of liability

19. The exclusion of liability might apply to the institution and its employees, so article 13 would read as follows:

"Save for intentional wrongdoing, the parties waive, to the fullest extent permitted under the applicable law, any claim against the mediator, [*name of the institution*] and its employees based on any act or omission in connection with the mediation."

III. Institutions administering mediation under the UNCITRAL Mediation Rules (2021) or providing some administrative and logistical services

20. The following remarks are intended to assist interested institutions in avoiding conflicts with the Rules in the administration of cases under the Rules or the provision of administrative and logistical services in relation to mediation under the Rules.

A. Administrative procedures or rules in conformity with the UNCITRAL Mediation Rules (2021)

21. In devising administrative procedures or rules, the institutions should have due regard to the interests of the parties. Since parties using the institutional services would have agreed that mediation is to be conducted under the Rules, their expectations should not be frustrated by practices or administrative rules that conflict with the Rules. Administering mediation under the Rules requires minimal adaptations, similar to those mentioned above in paragraphs 9–13. In this connection, it may be advisable that the institution clarify the role it will play by:

(a) Listing the administrative and logistical services offered; and/or

(b) Proposing to the parties a text of the UNCITRAL Mediation Rules (2021) highlighting the modifications made for the purpose of the administration of mediation; in this case, it is recommended that the institution indicates to potential users that the UNCITRAL Mediation Rules (2021) are "as administered by/amended by [*name of the institution*]" so that the user is made aware that the applicable rules are different to the UNCITRAL Mediation Rules (2021).

22. In addition, it is also recommended that:

(a) The administrative procedures of the institution distinguish clearly between the provision of administrative and logistical services and the provision of recommending and selecting a mediator under the UNCITRAL Mediation Rules (2021) (see chapter IV below), including a clear delineation between the services offered and, if charged, the related costs; and

(b) The institution indicates whether it is prepared to only administer mediation under the UNCITRAL Mediation Rules (2021) (and not leave a choice to the parties) or to also provide certain selected services of a technical and secretarial nature, which should be clearly described.

23. In setting out the administrative and logistical services that an institution offers, it is also recommended that the institution indicate:

(a) Which services are covered by which fee and which services would not be covered (that is, which would be billed separately) or whether the institution charges hourly fees;

(b) Which services are provided by its own staff and which are arranged to be provided by outside service providers; and

(c) That parties may also choose to have only a particular service (or services) provided by the institution without having the mediation fully administered by the institution.

B. Offer of administrative and logistical services

24. Article 4, paragraph 3 (b), provides that the parties, or the mediator with the consent of the parties, may arrange for administrative assistance. In this regard, institutions may consider providing the following non-exhaustive list of services as standing facilities or upon request:

(a) Maintenance of an online platform to facilitate administrative services with secure data protection and cybersecurity measures;

(b) Facilitating communication both in-person and virtually, including technical assistance during online mediations, taking into account the principles provided in the UNCITRAL Technical Notes on Online Dispute Resolution;[5]

(c) Providing secretarial or clerical assistance;

(d) Providing necessary practical arrangements for meetings, including:

(i) Assistance to the mediator in establishing the date, time and place of meetings;

(ii) Securing meeting rooms for in-person or hybrid (in-person and online) meetings during the mediation process;

(iii) Facilitating secured or encrypted telephone conference and videoconference facilities for remote or hybrid meetings;

(iv) Secretarial and clerical assistance in relation to meetings;

(v) Arranging for third-party services, including interpretation and translation;

(vi) Organizing, where possible, entry visas for the purpose of in-person meetings when mediation is carried out on the premises of the institution or in the same city in an outside facility;

(e) Attestation of settlement agreements in accordance with article 8 of the UNCITRAL Mediation Rules;[6]

(f) Translation of the settlement agreement; or

(g) Providing services with respect to the storage of settlement agreements and files relating to the mediation.

C. Administrative fee schedule

25. The institution, when indicating the fee or fees it charges for its services, if any, may reproduce its administrative fee schedule or, in the absence thereof, indicate the basis for calculating the fee or fees.

26. In view of the possible categories of services that an institution may offer, such as recommending and selecting the mediator or mediators and/or providing administrative and logistical services, it is recommended that the fee for each category be stated separately (see para. 22 (a) above).

[5] Facilitating communication could include ensuring that communications among parties and mediators are kept open and up to date and may also consist in merely forwarding written communications. It should also be noted that in accordance with article 4, paragraph 2 (a), of the Singapore Convention on Mediation, where a party requesting to rely on a settlement agreement concluded through electronic communications, the method used for the electronic communication shall meet certain criteria. Institutions may wish to follow these criteria in the method used for settlement agreements concluded through electronic communications.

[6] This provision mirrors both article 4, paragraph 1 (b) (iii), of the Singapore Convention on Mediation and article 18, paragraph 1 (b) (iii), of the 2018 Model Law on Mediation.

D. Draft model clauses

27. In the interest of procedural efficiency, institutions may wish to propose model mediation clauses covering the above services. It is recommended that:

(a) Where the institution fully administers mediation under the UNCITRAL Mediation Rules (2021), the model clause could read as follows:

"Any dispute, controversy, or claim arising out of or relating to this contract or the breach, termination, or invalidity thereof, shall be submitted to mediation in accordance with the UNCITRAL Mediation Rules (2021) administered by [*name of the institution*]."

(b) Where the institution provides certain mediation services only, the agreement as to the services that are requested should be indicated:

"Any dispute, controversy or claim arising out of or relating to this contract or the breach, termination, or invalidity thereof shall be submitted to mediation in accordance with the UNCITRAL Mediation Rules (2021). [*Name of institution*] shall assist the parties by recommending a prospective mediator and, if the parties cannot agree, select the mediator. [*Name of institution*] shall also provide administrative services in accordance with its administrative procedures for mediation proceedings under the UNCITRAL Mediation Rules (2021)."

(c) Where the institution fully administers mediation in the context of ongoing arbitration proceedings, the multi-tiered model clause could read as follows:

"If the parties, in the context of ongoing arbitration proceedings, wish to submit the dispute, or any part thereof, to mediation, then the parties agree that the dispute shall be submitted to mediation in accordance with the UNCITRAL Mediation Rules (2021) administered by [*name of institution*]."

(d) Where the institution would provide certain mediation services only in the context of ongoing arbitration proceedings, the multi-tiered model clause could read as follows:

"If the parties, in the context of ongoing arbitration proceedings, wish to submit the dispute, or any part thereof, to mediation, then the parties agree that the dispute shall be submitted to mediation in accordance with the UNCITRAL Mediation Rules (2021). [*Name of institution*] shall assist the parties by recommending and, if the parties cannot agree, selecting the mediator or mediators and providing administrative services in accordance with its administrative procedures for cases under the UNCITRAL Mediation Rules (2021)."

(e) In the above cases under subparagraphs (a)–(d), institutions may consider adding the following to the model clause:

"(i) The parties agree that there will be one mediator appointed by agreement of the parties [within thirty days of the mediation agreement];"

"(ii) The language of the mediation shall be [*language*];"

"(iii) The location of mediation shall be [*location*] [The mediation shall be performed remotely]."

(f) Where the institution would, in the event that mediation does not result in a settlement agreement, fully administer or provide certain services related to subsequent arbitration, the multi-tiered model clause could read as follows:

"If the dispute, or any part thereof, is not settled within [(60) days] of the request to mediate under the UNCITRAL Mediation Rules (2021), then the parties agree to resolve any remaining matters by arbitration in accordance with the [UNCITRAL Arbitration Rules (2021)] [*arbitration rules of* [*name of the institution*]]."

(g) In such cases, institutions may consider adding the following note:

"(i) The appointing authority shall be [*name of institution*];"

"(ii) The number of arbitrators shall be [one or three];"

"(iii) The place of arbitration shall be [*city and country*];"

"(iv) The language of the arbitration shall be [*language*]."

IV. Institutions recommending and selecting mediators

28. Article 3, paragraph 3, of the UNCITRAL Mediation Rules (2021) provides that parties can seek the assistance of an institution for the recommendation or selection of the mediator. Article 3, paragraphs 4 and 5, outline the considerations to which an institution should have regard in recommending or selecting individuals to act as mediators. Such considerations include:

(a) The professional expertise, language skills, and qualifications of the prospective mediator;

(b) Any relevant accreditation and/or certification awarded to the prospective mediator by a recognized professional mediation standards body;

(c) The availability of the prospective mediator;

(d) Elements likely to secure the appointment of an independent and impartial mediator;

(e) Elements likely to ensure diversity, including the nationality, gender or culture of the prospective mediator.

29. An institution that is willing and able to recommend and select mediators should describe the manner in which it will perform those functions (see para. 28 above) and the associated costs, if any.

Annex IV

List of documents before the Commission at its fifty-fifth session

Symbol	*Title or description*
A/CN.9/1083	Provisional agenda, annotations thereto and scheduling of meetings of the fifty-fifth session
A/CN.9/1084	Report of Working Group I (Micro-, Small and Medium-sized Enterprises) on the work of its thirty-sixth session
A/CN.9/1085	Report of Working Group II (Dispute Settlement) on the work of its seventy-fourth session
A/CN.9/1086	Report of Working Group III (Investor-State Dispute Settlement Reform) on the work of its forty-first session
A/CN.9/1087	Report of Working Group IV (Electronic Commerce) on the work of its sixty-second session
A/CN.9/1088	Report of Working Group V (Insolvency Law) on the work of its fifty-ninth session
A/CN.9/1089	Report of Working Group VI (Judicial Sale of Ships) on the work of its thirty-ninth session
A/CN.9/1090	Report of Working Group I (Micro-, Small and Medium-sized Enterprises) on the work of its thirty-seventh session
A/CN.9/1091	Report of the colloquium on possible future work on dispute settlement held during the seventy-fifth session of Working Group II
A/CN.9/1092	Report of Working Group III (Investor-State Dispute Settlement Reform) on the work of its forty-second session
A/CN.9/1093	Summary of the Chairperson and the Rapporteur of the work of Working Group IV (Electronic Commerce) at its sixty-third session
A/CN.9/1094	Report of Working Group V (Insolvency Law) on the work of its sixtieth session
A/CN.9/1095	Report of Working Group VI (Judicial Sale of Ships) on the work of its fortieth session
A/CN.9/1096	Bibliography of recent writings related to the work of UNCITRAL
A/CN.9/1097	Status of conventions and model laws and the operation of the Transparency Registry
A/CN.9/1098 and A/CN.9/1098/Corr.1	UNCITRAL regional presence
A/CN.9/1099	Technical cooperation and assistance
A/CN.9/1100	Dissemination of information and related activities to support the work of UNCITRAL and the use of its texts, including the report on CLOUT and digests
A/CN.9/1101	Results of the preparatory work by the UNCITRAL secretariat towards the development of a new international instrument on negotiable multimodal transport documents
A/CN.9/1102	Warehouse receipts
A/CN.9/1103	Work programme of the Commission
A/CN.9/1104	Relevant General Assembly resolutions
A/CN.9/1105	Role of UNCITRAL in promoting the rule of law at the national and international levels
A/CN.9/1106	International governmental and non-governmental organizations invited to sessions of UNCITRAL and its working groups

Symbol	*Title or description*
A/CN.9/1107	Coordination activities
A/CN.9/1108	Draft convention on the international effects of judicial sales of ships
A/CN.9/1109	Compilation of comments on the draft convention on the international effects of judicial sales of ships
A/CN.9/1109/Add.1	Compilation of comments: addendum 1
A/CN.9/1109/Add.2	Compilation of comments: addendum 2
A/CN.9/1109/Add.3	Compilation of comments: addendum 3
A/CN.9/1110	Draft explanatory note on the convention on the international effects of judicial sales of ships – part I
A/CN.9/1110/Add.1	Draft explanatory note – part II
A/CN.9/1110/Add.2	Draft explanatory note – part III
A/CN.9/1111	[*Not issued.*]
A/CN.9/1112	Draft model law on the use and cross-border recognition of identity management and trust services
A/CN.9/1113	Draft model law on the use and cross-border recognition of identity management and trust services: compilation of comments by Governments and international organizations
A/CN.9/1113/Add.1	Draft model law on the use and cross-border recognition of identity management and trust services: compilation of comments by Governments and international organizations – addendum 1
A/CN.9/1114	Early dismissal and preliminary determination
A/CN.9/1115	Endorsement of texts of other organizations: International Standard Demand Guarantee Practice for URDG 758
A/CN.9/1116	Legal issues related to digital economy – advancing work on automated contracting and other progress
A/CN.9/1117	Legal issues related to digital economy – proposal for future work on data transactions
A/CN.9/1118	Dispute settlement: recommendations to assist mediation centres and other interested bodies with regard to mediation under the UNCITRAL Mediation Rules (2021)
A/CN.9/1119	Exploratory work on the impact of the coronavirus disease (COVID-19) on international trade law
A/CN.9/1120	Possible future work on climate change mitigation, adaptation and resilience
A/CN.9/1120/Add.1	Possible future work on climate change mitigation, adaptation and resilience: addendum 1